ANTHOLOGY FOR MUSICAL ANALYSIS

Third Edition

ANTHOLOGY FOR MUSICAL ANALYSIS

Third Edition

Charles Burkhart

Queens College

HOLT, RINEHART AND WINSTON

New York · Chicago · San Francisco · Atlanta · Dallas · Montreal · Toronto

537880

Library of Congress Cataloging in Publication Data

Burkhart, Charles, musician.
  Anthology for musical analysis.

  1. Musical form.   2. Harmony.   I. Title.
MT58.B94   1979   781   78-15566

ISBN 0-03-018866-0

9 0 1   0 5 9   9 8 7 6 5 4 3 2 1

MT
58
B94
1979
cop. 2

Preface

This edition of *Anthology for Musical Analysis* is a collection of 194 complete compositions or movements ranging in time from the Middle Ages to 1978. While it is slightly larger than the second edition and contains a somewhat wider range of materials, the basic purposes of the book remain the same: to provide theory and musicianship classes on all levels with a large and varied body of material for analysis, playing, singing, transposing, and score-reading; and to provide sufficient material for both a full-year course in the analysis of musical forms and a one-semester course in twentieth-century techniques. The various uses of the book are facilitated by its two indexes, which enable teachers and students to quickly locate many specific examples of forms, genres, chords, sequences, modulations, and many other technical elements. Since the book consists primarily of music, and since it takes no theoretical position, it is adaptable to any theory of music and to any type of music theory curriculum.

The selections of music in this anthology favor those periods, composers, and genres that are most emphasized in theory and analysis courses. Though such a selection will necessarily contain a large amount of music for piano solo, over half the pieces in this book are for other media: There are 40 works for chorus or vocal ensemble (including 25 chorale harmonizations), 14 for solo voice and piano, 16 for small instrumental groups (including six movements for string quartet), and 5 orchestral movements in full score (plus a complete Handel aria with the accompaniment in score). Each is individually cited under "Media" in the General Index.

Organization of the Book

While many individual forms and techniques are represented by two or more examples chosen to display a progression from simple to complex, the book as a whole is not intended to be studied in a particular order. On the contrary, the basically chronological—and therefore neutral—arrangement leaves teachers free to choose the order that best suits their needs.

The 194 compositions by 48 composers are grouped in five large parts, each part devoted to a particular span of time. Within each part the composers represented are arranged by dates of birth. When more than one work of a composer is given, they are grouped by genre. An exception to the chronological arrangement is made for chorale harmonizations, which are all grouped together in an appendix.

Various teaching aids within the book are offered in lieu of a teacher's manual. First, each of the five large parts is preceded by an introduction giving a broad view of the contents and making suggestions for possible use. Likewise each composition (or group of similar compositions by one composer) is preceded by brief comments and questions for the student. The most comprehensive aids are the two indexes, the alphabetically arranged General Index and the systematically arranged Index of Chords, Sequences, and Modulations. Further directions on the indexes, together with some specific suggestions for their use, are given on the page preceding the General Index. The use of all these aids is, of course, optional. It is hoped they will promote fruitful exploration.

Special Features of the Third Edition

All five of the Anthology's parts and the Appendix have been slightly expanded. Of the total number of compositions, 27 percent are new. I have left intact what seemed to me the strongest areas of the book, and placed the majority of the changes in those parts that have proved less useful. The first part has been considerably revised with a view to greater practicality and diversity. Its new music includes a large selection of Gregorian chants. The Baroque and twentieth-century parts, while not so drastically revised, have also received a considerable number of new pieces. In the latter, major additions are Ives's song, *General William Booth Enters into Heaven*, and the first movement of Bartók's *Music for Strings, Percussion and Celesta*. In designing this edition, the opinions and suggestions of many teachers have been of help in selecting some new pieces, and also led me to reinstate three selections included in the first edition but dropped in the second: *all* movements of Beethoven's *String Quartet*, Op. 135, Schoenberg's song, *Sommermüd*, and Theme with Variations from Stravinsky's *Sonata for Two Pianos*.

A constant goal throughout this revision has been to provide more elementary material without serious detriment to the body of advanced material. Among the most elementary new pieces are the first of the Susato dance pairs, the Handel *Chaconne*, three more pieces from the Anna Magdalena Notebook, the Clementi *Sonatina*, Brahms's Wiegenlied, and the Krenek *Suite for Violoncello Solo*, first movement.

More orchestral scores have also been included in response to many requests. New items are the movement from the second "Brandenburg" concerto, the minuet from Haydn's *Symphony No. 101*, and the first movement from Bartók's *Music for Strings, Percussion and Celesta*. Another new feature is the inclusion of *sample pages of the full score* of two orchestral works retained from the second edition and given in piano arrangement. Another retained work, the first movement of Mozart's piano concerto, K. 491, is now given *in full score*. And the score of the finale of Haydn's *Symphony No. 101* now appears in a size that makes it much easier to read.

Four other features have been added to increase the usefulness or convenience of the book in the classroom: The commentary and questions have been almost entirely rewritten with a view to greater clarity; the indexes have been improved; several pieces with figured bass have been provided with an extra staff for writing in the realization; and spiral binding lets the book lie open more easily on desk or piano.

I hope those who use this book will not view the music it contains merely as *examples* of a particular form or technique. To do so would be to lose the ultimate point of studying a piece of music at all, which is to deepen one's esthetic response to that particular work. I have tried to select pieces that are not only clear examples, but are also of an artistic quality that will reward the student as only a great piece of music can.

I am deeply indebted to the many colleagues and friends who have discussed this revision with me. Particular thanks are due Prof. Douglass Green of the University of Texas at Austin for his many excellent suggestions on the book as a whole, and Susan Hellauer, my colleague at Queens College, for her generous assistance on Part One. In a realm beyond grateful acknowledgment is the help given me throughout by my wife, Marian.

The contributions of the following are also very much appreciated: Thomas Trobaugh, University of Wisconsin/Milwaukee; David S. Lewis, Ohio University; William Duckworth, Bucknell University; H. Richard Hensel, Eastern Kentucky University; Harry Jacobson, University of Tennessee; Allen O. Breach, Howard University; Randall Shinn, University of New Orleans; David T. Childs, Wichita State University; Leonard Berkowitz, California State University/Northridge; Ramiro Cortes, University of Utah; Preston Stedman, California State University/Fullerton; Tim Blickhan, Northern Illinois University; Pete De-Lone, Indiana University; Bruce Archibald, Temple University; Jack Johnston, University of South Carolina; Dennis Kam, University of Miami; Robert Beadell, University of Nebraska/Lincoln; John Rogers, University of New Hampshire; Jerry Dean, University of Texas/Austin; Thomas Benjamin, University of Houston; Lee Humphries, University of Minnesota/Minneapolis; Moonyeen Albrecht, Central Michigan University; Luther Stripling, Macalester College; Kenneth R. Rumery, Northern Arizona University; and Bruce Saylor, New York University.

CHARLES BURKHART

New York
January 1979

Contents

PART TWO Late Baroque Compositions

PART THREE *Classical Compositions*

PART FOUR Compositions of the Romantic Era

APPENDIX *Chorale Harmonizations*
by Johann Sebastian Bach and several of his predecessors
(by Bach unless otherwise indicated)

ANTHOLOGY
FOR
MUSICAL
ANALYSIS
Third Edition

PART ONE

From Chant to Early Baroque

This selection of mostly pre-Baroque music is designed, like the book as a whole, with the needs of theory and analysis students in mind. It does not pretend to answer the needs of history classes that genuinely attempt to do justice to the great heritage of medieval and Renaissance music, and it intentionally avoids (with one exception) the duplication of pieces given in that rich and irreplaceable book, Davison and Apel's *Historical Anthology of Music*, Volume I.

The ten examples of plainchant that open Part One provide a variety of problems in the analysis of melody and form. Also, together with certain of the polyphonic pieces, they have been chosen to exemplify the attributes of the various ecclesiastical modes. Since the modes used are not specified, the examples can be used for modal analysis, whatever position one takes on the relevance of modal theory to musical practice or on the relation of modality to tonality; and the way is left open for discussion of how the students hear the piece in terms of a "tonal center."

At one time the music of Palestrina was held up as the sole model for students of counterpoint. Later, the polyphony of Lassus and some other late Renaissance composers came to be deemed equally valuable. In today's broad approach, this repertoire no longer holds first place, but it remains one of several high points in the history of musical style and structure. The late Renaissance examples here not only show a variety of contrapuntal techniques, but also progress in complexity from the 2-part *Cantiones* of Lassus, through the simple 3-part madrigal of Wilbye and the more florid 3-part and 4-part Palestrina examples to the 6-part anthem of Gibbons. But not all the polyphonic examples are in imitative counterpoint. The Dufay *fauxbourdon* and especially the first Susato dance pair are relevant to the study of elementary harmony (as are the seven items in the Appendix, page 593 by Renaissance and early Baroque composers).

While primary emphasis here is on the individual work and the value of concentrated study of it, the comparing of *several* works, perhaps from different periods, that share some technique or form is certainly interesting and can also be of value when not allowed to become simplistic. (It is not *forbidden* to gain some historical perspective from an analysis anthology!) For example, very different *cantus-firmus* techniques are exemplified in Part One by the isorhythmic motets, the Dufay *Communio*, the Desprez canon, and the Palestrina *Sanctus* and *Benedictus*. These might in turn be compared with the use of cantus firmus in the Bach chorale preludes (especially *Vor deinen Tron*) given in Part Two. Consider as well the use of pre-existent material in Charles Ives's "General William Booth Enters into Heaven." How is this usage different? Is it *cantus firmus* technique? Also, Part One provides five pieces called "motet" that are quite removed from one another in time and very different in construction and style. Likewise the Desprez canon may be compared with the canons in Part Two from the *Musical Offering* and with the one in Part Five by Stravinsky. (All items are cited by page in the General Index.) And the works employing canonic imitation clearly are related to later imitative pieces such as the Corelli *Preludio* and the Baroque fugues—especially the ricercar-like fugues in C major and D sharp minor from the *Well-tempered Clavier*. Finally, the treatment of the *color* of Machaut's isorhythmic motet might be contrasted with that of the tone row of Krenek's cello piece.

More challenging than facile comparisons of a particular genre or form as it changes from age to age are historical comparisons that involve analysis of finer details. One such is suggested by the late Renaissance examples of extreme chromaticism given in Part One, particularly the Prologue to the *Prophetiae Sibyllarum* of Lassus. What is the difference between the chromaticism here and that in, say, Bach's harmonizations of *Valet will ich dir geben* (page 617) and *Es ist genug* (page 603)? Another is afforded by juxtaposing Monteverdi's *Lasciatemi morire* with the Palestrina *Sanctus* or with *Tu pauperum refugium* of Desprez. Exactly how does the revolutionary *seconda prattica* depart from the "old style," so staunchly defended by the conservatives of the time?

Examples of Plainchant[1]

The following chants, all in musically complete form, provide for the analysis of Gregorian melody and modality.[2] Identify the mode in each case. Does the *finalis* always sound like a tonic? If not, can one hear it as such? Do modulations occur? Consider what factors create the feeling of a tonal center. Also examine the motivic content and musical form of each example. (Two additional chants will be found on pages 18 and 33.) The first example, besides being given in modern notation, is also given as it appears in the *Liber Usualis*.

Kyrie from Mass XI ("Orbis factor") (LU 46)

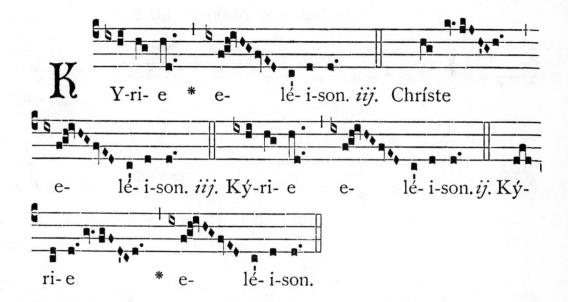

---

[1]Beside the title of each example is the page on which the chant will be found in the *Liber Usualis* (LU), *with Introduction and Rubrics in English*, edited by the Benedictines of Solesmes (Desclée, Tournai, 1938). These examples have been rendered into modern notation by Susan Hellauer.

[2]A classic discussion of the modal system and the forms of Gregorian chant is that of Gustave Reese in his *Music in the Middle Ages* (Norton, 1940). See his page 152 for a useful diagram on modal classification.

Ky - ri - e e - le - i - son *(2x)*

Ky - ri - e e - le - i - son.

Lord, have mercy,
Christ, have mercy,
Lord, have mercy.

Sanctus from Mass II (LU 21)

San - ctus ✸ san - ctus san - ctus

Do - mi - nus De - us Sa - ba - oth. Ple - ni sunt cae - li et ter - ra

glo - ri - a tu - a. Ho - san - na in ex - cel - sis.

Be - ne - dic - tus qui ve - nit in no - mi - ne

Do - mi - ni. Ho - san - na in ex - cel - sis.

"Holy, holy, holy, Lord God of hosts. Heaven and earth are full of thy glory. Hosanna in the highest. Blessed is he that cometh in the name of the Lord. Hosanna in the highest."

Tone for the "Benedicamus Domino" (LU 124)

Be - ne - di - ca - mus Do -

mi - no.

"Let us bless the Lord. Thanks be to God."

Hymn to St. John the Baptist (LU 1504)

Ut que-ant lax - is re - so - na - re fi - bris Mi - ra ges - to - rum

fa - mu - li tu - o - rum, Sol - ve pol - lu - ti la - bi - i re - a - tum, Sanc - te Jo - an - nes.

(Four more verses follow to identical music.—For a translation and the historical significance of this famous hymn, see Reese, *Middle Ages,* pp. 149–150.)

Hymn for Lauds, December 25 (LU 400)

A so - lis or - tus car - di - ne Ad us - que ter - rae li - mi - tem,

Chris - tum ca - na - mus Prin - ci - pem, Na - tum Ma - ri - a Vir - gi - ne.

"At the rising of the sun, Unto the limits of the earth, Let us sing Christ the Prince, Born of the Virgin Mary."

Agnus Dei from Mass I (LU 18)

A - gnus De - i, qui tol - lis pec - ca - ta mun - di:
A - gnus De - i, qui tol - lis pec - ca - ta mun - di:

mi - se - re -   re   no -   bis. *(2x)*
do - na   no -   bis   pa -   cem.

"Lamb of God, who takest away the sins of the world, have mercy on us." *(Twice)*
"Lamb of God, who takest away the sins of the world, grant us peace."

Gradual for the Second Sunday of Lent (LU 546)

Tri-bu-la - ti-o - nes   * cor - dis me - i

di - la - ta - tae   sunt: de   ne-ces-si -

ta - ti - bus   me - is   e - ri-pe me,

Do -   mi - ne.

℣. Vi -   de hu - mi -

li - ta - tem   me - am,   et la-bo -

rem me - um: et di - mit-te

om - ni - a   pec - ca - ta ✳

me - a.

"The troubles of my heart are multiplied: deliver me from my necessities, O Lord. See my abjection and my labor, and forgive me all my sins." (*Psalms 24:17–18, Douay*)

Communion for the Midnight Mass of Christmas (LU 395)

In splen-do - ri-bus ✳ sanc - to - rum, ex u - te - ro

an - te lu - ci - fe - rum   ge - nu - i - te.

(For translation and musical significance, see Reese, *Middle Ages,* p. 160.)

Introit for the Feast of St. John of Damascus (LU 1418)

Te - nu - i - sti ✳ ma - num dex - te-ram me - am:

et in vo-lun-ta - te tu - a   de -du - xis -ti   me,

et cum glo-ri - a   su - sce - pi-sti me

Ps. Quam bo - nus Is - ra-el De - us, ✳ his qui rec - to sunt cor - de!

"Thou hast held me by my right hand, and by thy will thou hast conducted me, and with thy glory thou hast received me." *(Psalms 72: 24, Douay)*

Psalm: "How good is God to Israel, to them that are right of heart." *(Psalms 72: 1, Douay)* "Glory be to the Father, and to the Son, and to the Holy Ghost. As it was in the beginning, is now, and ever shall be, world without end. Amen."

Tract for Holy Saturday, "Sicut cervus" (LU 753)

ci - em De - i me-i?

𝒱. Fu - e - runt mi - hi la-cri-mae me - ae

pa -nes di-e ac noc - te, dum di - ci -

tur mi - hi per sin-gu -los di - es:

u - bi est ✻ De - us tu - us?

"As the hart panteth after the fountains of water, so my soul panteth after thee, O God. My soul hath thirsted for the living God: when shall I come and appear before the face of God? My tears have been my bread day and night, while they say to me daily: Where is thy God?" (*Psalms 41: 2-4, Douay*)

Motet: *Las!—Donés sui—EIUS*

Anonymous
(between ca. 1225–1260)

The isorhythmic motet flourished in France in the thirteenth and fourteenth centuries. This example, the first of two, is of a type known as the Parisian motet; the second, given on page 12, is considerably later and more elaborate.[3]

In the isorhythmic motet, which was typically in three voices, the lowest voice, or *tenor*, was constructed of a series of pitches (called the *color*) taken from a plainchant. This series was subjected to an "isorhythm," that is, a constantly reiterated rhythmic pattern (called the *talea*). In *Las!—Donés sui—EIUS*, the color is the tenor's first 25 notes. Notice that the entire series is repeated once. The talea is the 5-note pattern: 𝄴 ♩ ♪♪ 𝄾 | ♩. ♩ 𝄾 | How many times is it repeated? This color comes from the responsory *Stirps Jesse* (in honor of the Blessed Virgin Mary), being the notes of the melisma on the single, and final, word *"eius."*[4] The melisma happens to be identical with one in the tone for *Benedicamus Domino* given on page 5. See the melisma there on the word "Domino" and compare it with the tenor of this motet.

Such pieces were composed from the bottom up. The tenors, which were usually given no additional text, may have been vocalized in the earliest motets; later they may have come to be performed instrumentally. The upper parts were both vocal, and each was given a different, and secular, text. The whole was a sophisticated union of sacred and secular intended for the delectation of highly cultivated listeners.

Study the upper parts as well as the tenor of this example. How are phrases articulated? What kinds of vertical sonorities and chords are favored? In what contexts do dissonances occur? And consonances? To what extent are complete triads used?

[3]The origin and early development of the motet are discussed in Reese, *Middle Ages*, p. 311f. See also Richard Crocker, *A History of Musical Style* (New York: McGraw-Hill, 1966), p. 91f., for a treatment of the Parisian motet in particular.

[4]See *Antiphonale Romanum*, Appendix, Cantus varii, "In honorem B. Mariae Virginae."

Triplum

Alas! since I have come to know
The Beauty fair of face
For whom I pine,
Now seems it that I
Her slave must be
With full loyal heart?
Lo! at the vision of her beauty,
Her grace, her charm, her sweet smile,
More am I by love o'ercome.
Without her comfort
To death must I go;
I beg that she have pity
On her faithful friend.

Motetus

I am given up without regret
To my beloved friend,
To love and serve her
In no way foolishly.
I cry to her for mercy,
Like her very gentle friends;
For her love I pine and die.
So worthy is my lady [that]
Of all ills she can heal me.
If I love the Beauty of the world,
Then all the world must praise me.

(*Trans. by Margaret Webb*)

Motet: *De bon espoir—Puisque la douce rousee—SPERAVI*

(mid-fourteenth century)

Guillaume de Machaut

(ca. 1300–1377)

The isorhythmic principle is here realized in a more highly developed manner than in the previous example, which is recommended to be studied first.

In this motet the color is taken from a Gregorian *introit* beginning with the words, "Domine, in tua misericordia speravi" (Lord, in thy mercy I hoped).[5] The word "speravi" is set in the chant as follows:

spe - - - ra - - vi.

Locate all statements of both color and talea, and analyze the relationship of the two. Notice that the upper parts also display considerable rhythmic repetition. Compare their rhythms with the rhythmic structure of the tenor. In spite of its many fixed elements, this piece also produces considerable variety. How so? What keeps changing rather than repeating?

Much remains uncertain about the original style of performance of fourteenth-century motets. Today, the tenor is usually played on an instrument, and the upper parts are sometimes instrumentally doubled at the unison or the higher octave. It is suggested that the tempo of this motet flow at a fairly quick pace, perhaps at one to the ⁶⁄₈ bar. One must beware of assuming that the words suggest a particular interpretation, as in the vocal music of later eras. But apropos of the words themselves, notice here how the theme of hope (*espoir*) is reflected in the choice of cantus firmus, which says: "I hoped" (*speravi*). (Though the term "motet" has endured to the present day, the fourteenth-century motet was something quite different from the motets of later times. Later examples will be found on pages 20 , 39 , and 62 .)

Reprinted by permission of the publisher, Éditions de l'Oiseau-Lyre, Monaco, from *Polyphonic Music of the Fourteenth Century*, vol. 3, ed. Leo Schrade. Copyright 1956.

[5]See *Graduale Romanum*, first Sunday after Pentecost.

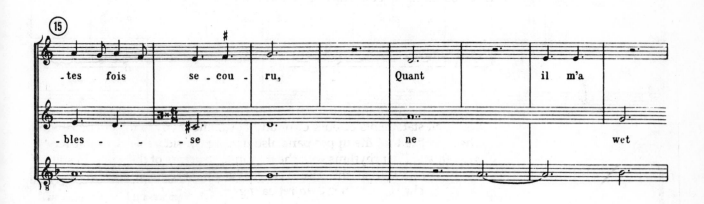

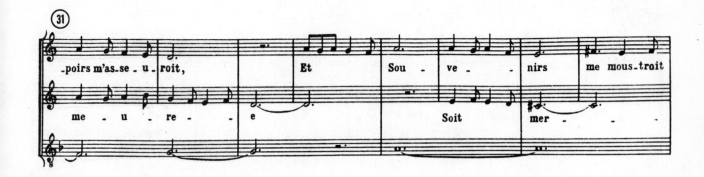

Triplum

By Good Hope, by Very Sweet Remembrance,
And by Very Gentle Thought has good Love
Oft times been help to me against Desire
When he with utmost strength assailed me;
And the more that Desire has tortured me,
Most gently Hope has reassured me,
And Remembrance showed to me the beauty,
The sense, honor, value, and the goodness
Of the one about whom a tender thought
Came to give comfort to my mourning heart.

Alas! then did Desire e'en more assail,
But strong resistance to him saved me,
Though I was near to losing the comfort
Of Good Hope, which would destroy my courage.
And Mem'ry makes me always remember
When my sad heart would force me to despair.
For Grace, and Love, and Faith, and Loyalty,
Compassion, Learning, and Nobility
In me alone now soundly are asleep;
For Danger reigns above the power of Grace;
And since my lady, to whom I am bound,

Believes in Hardness and proud Refusal,
And wants this, not my love nor my heart,
I cannot leave, whate'er the cost.

Still, since it cannot now be otherwise,
Let her make of me whatsoe'er she will;
In spite of it I'll love her faithfully.

Motetus
Now since the sweet dew
Of humility does not wish to make
Pity bloom until it ripens,
Thanks be I may not achieve
What I so much desire;
For in me is engendered,
By an amorous desire,
An ardor beyond measuring

That Love, by its sweet pleasure,
And my desired lady,
By her most brilliant beauty,
Through grace have aroused in me.
But since thus they be pleased,
I wish humbly to endure
What they will until I die.

(*Trans. by Margaret Webb*)

Communio

from *Missa Sancti Jacobi*

(ca. 1428)

Guillaume Dufay

(ca. 1400–1474)

Dufay's *Missa Sancta Jacobi*, which contains settings of both Proper and Ordinary, concludes with this *Communio*.[6] An early example of *fauxbourdon*, it was originally notated on two staves with instructions that a third voice should duplicate the top voice a perfect fourth lower. What makes this composition more than a mere succession of parallel $^6_3$ chords? Also analyze the relation of the piece to the chant on which it is based.

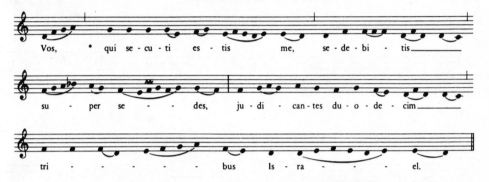

You, who have followed me, shall sit on seats judging the twelve tribes of Israel.
(*St. Matthew 19:28, Douay Version.*)

An interpretive question is whether or not the six quarter notes of each bar are consistently felt as two groups of three, as implied by the modern time signature. A tempo of about 63 to the dotted half note is suggested.

[6]Gustave Reese discusses the historical importance of this movement as well as the fauxbourdon as a genre in *Music in the Renaissance* (New York: W. W. Norton, rev. ed., 1959), pp. 64f.

Tu pauperum refugium

Motet for Four Voices

(late fifteenth century)

Josquin Desprez[7]

(ca. 1440–1521)

Although this composition is the second unit of a large bipartite work, *Magnus es tu, Domine*, it forms a complete entity. Investigate the sensitively balanced phrases of unequal length and, in particular, the chordal and melodic structure of each phrase. The work is a rich example of the characteristics of the Phrygian mode. What "key" areas other than E are favored?

The text falls into two large parts that separate at the end of bar 33. How does the music express this two-part form?[8]

Thou art refuge of the poor, alleviator of weakness, hope of the exiled, strength of the burdened, path for the wandering, truth, and life.

And now, O Lord Redeemer, to thee alone I flee; I adore thee as the true God, in thee I hope, in thee I trust, O Jesus Christ, my salvation. Help me, lest my soul should ever sleep in death.

Reprinted by permission of the publishers from Archibald T. Davison and Willi Apel, eds., *Historical Anthology of Music*, Vol. 1, Cambridge, Mass.: Harvard University Press. Copyright 1946, 1949, by the President and Fellows of Harvard College.

[7] The attribution of this work to Josquin, while traditional, is not certain.

[8] Felix Salzer and Carl Schachter give a detailed analysis of this work in *Counterpoint in Composition* (New York: McGraw-Hill, 1969), pp. 402–409.

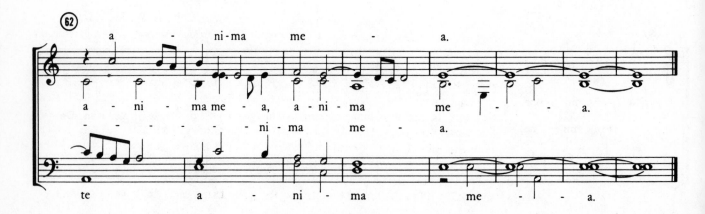

Baises moy

(publ. 1502)

Josquin Desprez

(ca. 1440–1521)

Before looking at the composition below, sing this fifteenth-century folk song:

"Bai - sés moy, bai - sés moy! Bai-sés moy, ma doulce a - my - e.

Par a-mour je vous em - pri - e." "Non fe - ray."

"Et pour - quoy?" "Se je fai-sois la fol - li - e.

Ma mè-re se-roit mar - ri - e." "Ve - la de quoy! Ve - la de quoy!"

"Kiss me, kiss me, my sweet; for love I pray you."
"I won't."
"And why?"
"If I committed such folly, Mama would be angry. That's why."

Now observe how Josquin has treated this tune in the following 4-voice set-ting. And ponder the fact that all these fixed melodic elements fit together so neatly within the constraints of triadic harmony.

What is the interval of imitation in this piece? There would seem to be a possible connection between this interval and the interesting fact that only *two* of the four parts bear a signature of one flat. (What is the connection?) And could this fact, in turn, at least suggest that the canonic imitation should be not tonal but real—that is, at exactly the same interval throughout? At any rate, notice how the editor of of the version we print here has solved, for reasons of his own, the problem of *musica ficta*. (See *A Note on the Sources*, page 622.)

Josquin's little piece, an amusing marriage of popular and high art, was likely written to be performed by instruments. Take it at a merry clip, two to the bar.

Superius

Altus

Tenor

Bassus

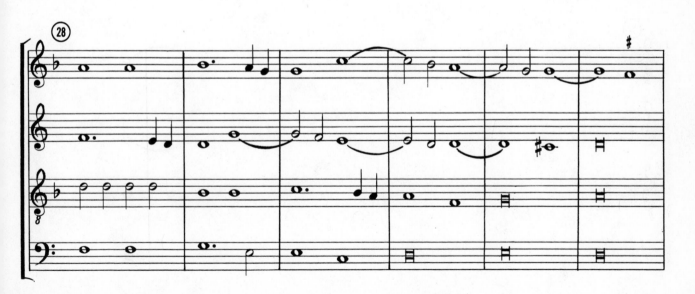

Two Dance Pairs

(publ. 1551)

Tielman Susato

(died ca. 1561)

Around 1540 the Belgian trumpeter and composer, Tielman Susato, established himself as a printer of music in Antwerp. His excellent publications of both sacred and secular works by many composers of the Low Countries remain an important primary source of the music of his time. In 1551 he brought out *Het derde musyck boexcken* (*The Third Little Music Book*), a collection of instrumental dances. Many of these are arrangements, likely by Susato himself, of popular dance tunes. In accord with sixteenth-century practice, this book specifies no instrumentation, a matter to be worked out by the players with whatever means were available. Doubtless many of the dances were performed on wind instruments at festive outdoor gatherings.

The Little Music Book gives several examples of the traditional sixteenth-century genre, the "dance pair," that is, two versions of the same tune played one after the other. In such a pair the first dance (the *Tanz*) was in slow or moderate duple time, the second, (the *Nachtanz* or "after-dance,") in quick triple time. Frequently, the meter of the two dances was in the proportion of 2 to 3. Such is the case in both of the pairs given below: The ♩ of the *tanz* is equivalent in duration to the ♩. of the *Nachtanz*. (For further examples of proportional tempi, see Elliott Carter's *Canaries*, page 570.)

Ronde—Hupfauf

Notice how this lively round dance with "Hop Up" is composed almost wholly of a few triads in root position. In the *Nachtanz*, exactly how are the duple rhythms turned into triple? (Compare Variation 12 of the Mozart work starting on page 202.)

Hupfauf

Pavane—Galliarde

This pair is subtitled "Die Herrin" (The Lady), likely a dance tune. How is the galliarde similar to the pavane? The pitch level given here follows the original, which must have been intended for low instruments. Of course, the entire piece can be played an octave higher or in a different key.

Galliarde

Sanctus and Benedictus

from *Missa Aeterna Christi Munera*

(publ. 1590)

Giovanni Pierluigi da Palestrina

(ca. 1525–1594)

In our time, which prizes originality so highly, it is difficult to realize how willingly some Renaissance composers based their works on previously composed music. Of Palestrina's 105 masses, 52 are re-workings, or "parodies," of earlier polyphonic compositions by Palestrina himself or by others; in most of the rest, plainchant provides the pre-existent material. Less than ten are entirely original.

Of the chant-based masses, 34 are in a special class in which the given chant, rather than being confined to the tenor voice and explicitly stated there, appears in paraphrased fragments in *all* the voices. The *Missa Aeterna Christi Munera* is such a "paraphrase mass." It is based on a chant of that name which in Palestrina's time was the matins hymn for the Common of Apostles. We give it here in a version used during the sixteenth century:

Ae - ter - na Chri - sti mu - - ne - ra, A - po - sto - lo - rum glo - ri - am,
Lau - des ca - nen - tes de - bi - tas, Lae - tis ca - na - mus men - - ti - bus.

[Let us sing] the eternal gifts of Christ
and the glory of the apostles—
[these,] the praises that we owe,
with happy minds let us sing.

This music poses several quite different analytic problems. One is to discover the manifold variants of the phrases of the chant that permeate almost every bar. Another is to deduce precisely how Palestrina treated dissonance in relation to rhythm; his style is extremely consistent in this respect. A more general problem is to locate the canonic imitations, noting their relation to the large sections of each movement and to the text. Finally, consider the question: What aspects of this music are original?

Sanctus

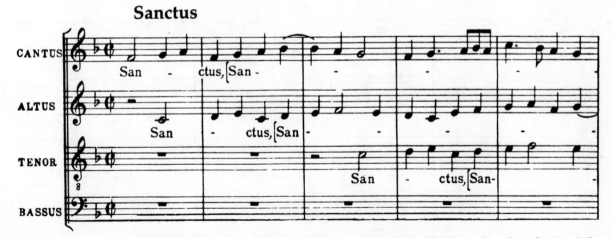

Reprinted by permission of the Institute Italiano per la Storia della Musica from *Opere Complete di G. P. da Palestrina*, Vol. 15, Raffaele Casimiri, ed.

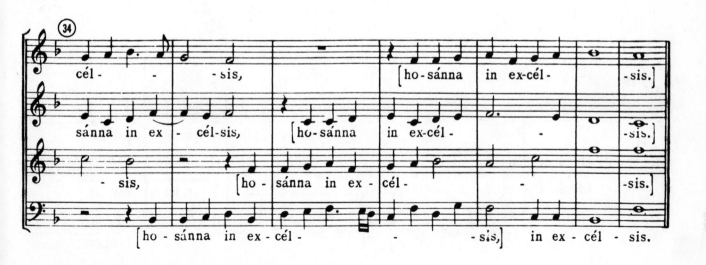

Benedictus

-mi-ni, [in nó-mi-ne Dó- -mi-ni.]

-mi-ni,] in nó-mi-ne Dó- -mi-ni.

mi-ne Dó- -mi-ni,] in nó-mi-ne Dó-mi-ni.

CANTUS

Ho-sánna in ex-cél-

ALTUS

Ho-sánna in ex-cél-

TENOR

Ho-sánna in ex-cél-

BASSUS

Ho-sánna in ex-cél - sis,

-sis, [ho-sánna in ex-cél-

sis, [ho-sánna in ex-cél-

-sis, [ho-sánna in ex-cél-

[ho- sánna in ex-cél - sis,]

Cantiones Duarum Vocum

Nos. 1, 6, and 11

(publ. 1577)

Roland de Lassus

(1532–1594)

Though Lassus' twelve motets for two voices have long served as models to students of counterpoint, they are not merely schoolbook illustrations, but little masterpieces of their genre. The *Cantiones* may also be viewed as typical of the state of modality in late sixteenth-century sacred music. How close are they to major and minor? Though modal, do these pieces have tonal centers, modulations? In what terms can one analyze their form? In the many canonic imitations, what factors have an effect on whether an imitation is tonal or real?

1—Beatus vir

Blessed is the man that shall continue in wisdom, and that shall meditate in his justice, and in his mind shall think of the all seeing eye of God.

(Ecclesiasticus 14:22, Douay Version.)

6—Qui sequitur me

He that followeth me, walketh not in darkness, but shall have the light of life: saith the Lord.

(St. John 8:12, Douay Version.)

Cantus
Qui se - qui-tur me, qui se - qui-tur me, qui se -

Altus
Qui se - qui-tur me, qui se - qui-tur me, qui

- qui-tur me,_____ non am - bu - lat, non am - bu -
se - qui-tur me,_____ non am - bu - lat, non am -

lat in_____ te - ne - bris,_____
- bu - lat in_____ te - ne - bris, sed__

11—Fulgebunt justi

The righteous shall blossom like the lily, and like the rose of Jericho shall they flower before the Lord.

Prologue to *Prophetiae Sibyllarum*

(1550–1552)

Roland de Lassus

(1532–1594)

The *Sibylline Oracles,* written in Greek hexameters by various poets between the second century B.C. and the fifth century A.D., include some poems that treat the subject of the advent of Christ as though foretold by the sibyls. These ancient texts appealed to the imagination of the young Roland de Lassus, who composed his *Prophetiae Sibyllarum* to Latin translations of twelve of them, depicting their "prophetic" quality by the use of bold, often baffling chromaticism. The portion quoted here is the short Prologue to the work, for which Lassus himself may have composed the words.

The ultimate question about the music of this prologue, not to mention the motets that follow it, is how one hears it with respect to tonality. Is it in C with an ending on the dominant, or in G with an opening on the subdominant, or does it hover ambiguously between two or more "tonics?" Or is it atonal? If so, are its pitches organized in any detectable systematic way? How is the chromaticism regulated from chord to chord? (At bar 24, the tenor singer was quite possibly expected to raise his F to an F♯.)[9]

This example may be compared with the Gesualdo madrigal on page 47. Which makes the more radical use of chromaticism?

> The songs you hear sung in a chromatic way—these are they in which the mysteries of our salvation were long ago foretold with fearless mouths by the twice-six sibyls.

Reproduced from *Das Chorwerk,* Vol. 48, p. 5, Friedrich Blume, editor. Copyright 1937 by Georg Kallmeyer, Berlin, Reprinted by permission of the present copyright owner, *Möseler Verlag Wolfenbüttel.*

[9]Opposing views of this work are offered by Edward E. Lowinsky in *Tonality and Atonality in Sixteenth-Century Music* (Berkeley: University of California Press, 1961), pp. 39–41, and William Mitchell in "The Prologue to Orlando di Lasso's Prophetiae Sibyllarum," an article in Vol. II, pp. 264–273, of *The Music Forum* (New York: Columbia University Press, 1970).

Moro lasso al mio duolo

Madrigal for five voices
(1611)

Carlo Gesualdo
(ca. 1560–1613)

The astonishing chromaticism of this madrigal, like that of the Lassus piece on the previous page, raises fundamental questions about pitch organization in music. While it is true that the form of the text is reflected in the music, one must also ask to what extent this piece is held together and given coherence by purely musical forces.

I die, alas! from my pain,
And the one who can give me life,
Alas, kills me and will not give me life.

I die, alas! from my pain,
And the one who can give me life,
Alas, kills me and will not give me aid.

O grievous fate,
The one who can give me life,
Alas, gives me death.

Reprinted from *A Treasury of Early Music,* compiled and edited with notes by Carl Parrish. By permission of W. W. Norton & Company, Inc. Copyright 1958 by W. W. Norton & Company, Inc.

Lasciatemi morire
from the Sixth Book of Madrigals for Five Voices
(publ. 1614)

Claudio Monteverdi
(1567-1643)

Text: Ottavio Rinuccini

Lasciatemi morire is the first of four madrigals that together comprise a larger work entitled *Lamento d'Arianna*. Originally the *Lamento* was composed as a monody (for solo voice and continuo) and occurred in the opera *Arianna* (1608), a work of which only fragments have survived. Monteverdi later arranged the *Lamento* in madrigal form.

The radical change in musical style that took place in Monteverdi's time is vividly reflected in his own compositions, which he himself distinguished as composed in either the old style (*prima prattica*) or the new (*seconda prattica*). As often happens when traditions are modified, this shift in style gave rise to heated polemics.[10] A characteristic of the new style—and one particularly offensive to Monteverdi's critics—was its way of treating dissonance. Examine the use of dissonance throughout *Lasciatemi morire* and compare it with that of compositions typical of the old style, for example, the Palestrina mass excerpt beginning on page 33, or the Desprez motet on page 20.

Another feature of the new style was the intimate relation of the music to the words. In this madrigal, how does the music express the meaning of the words?

[O,] let me die.
[For] who could comfort me
  in my hard fate,
  in my great martyrdom?

[10]See the famous attack by the conservative theorist, G. M. Artusi, which, together with Monteverdi's defense, is given in English translation in Strunk, *Source Readings in Music History* (Norton, 1950), pp. 393–412. Artusi's critique is very instructive on certain technical differences between the old and new styles.

As Fair as Morn

from *Second Set of Madrigals to 3, 4, 5, and 6 Parts Apt Both for Voyals and Voyces*

(publ. 1609)

John Wilbye

(1574–1638)

This mock-serious madrigal provides a fairly simple example of three-part imitative counterpoint. (Another example, but a very different one, is the Palestrina *Benedictus* on page 36).

The lowest part, originally notated in the tenor clef, is given here in the treble clef. Wilbye intended it for tenor voice, but a low alto also can sing it.

Hosanna to the Son of David
Anthem for Six Voices

Orlando Gibbons
(1583–1625)

Text based on St. Matthew 21:9 and St. Luke 19:38.

The anthem is a motet with English words. An outgrowth of the Reformation in England, the anthem soon established its own individuality. However, many anthems, including this famous example, share some general stylistic features with continental sacred music of the late Renaissance. One of these is imitation in points, which here luxuriates in six independent parts. Compare the use of points in the Palestrina and Lassus works on pages 33 and 39.

Analyze the form of this composition. Besides point imitation, what other means are used to articulate sections? How do the sections relate to each other? In the absence of tempo and dynamic marks, consider how a conductor might interpret this piece to achieve a clear and convincing projection of its structure. An unusual scoring occurs in bars 1 through 7 and in one other place, where the bottom two of the six voices are not the normal tenor and bass, but the tenors divided into two parts. Study these passages and discover the musical logic of this scoring.

An organ part exists in some sources of this work, but since it does little more than double the voices, it is omitted here. The work is often performed *a cappella*. Also, it is sung as much as a major third higher, since the original key is low in terms of modern pitch and modern choruses.

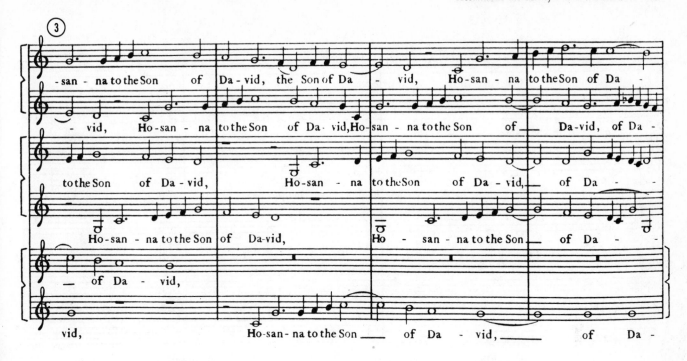

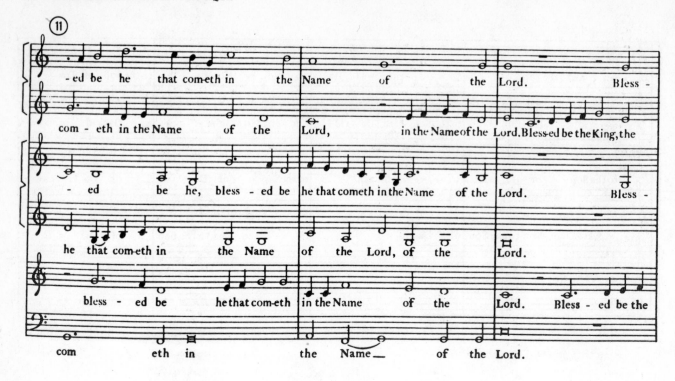

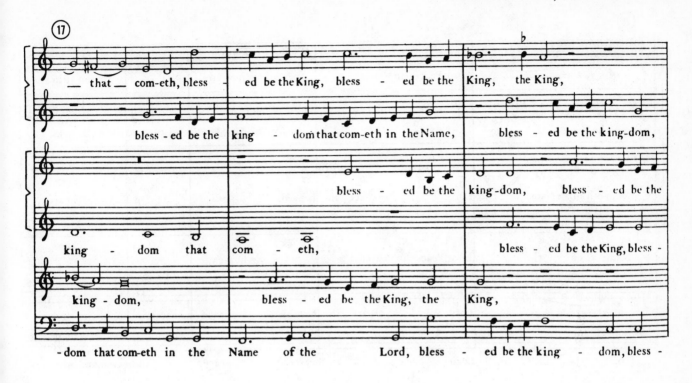

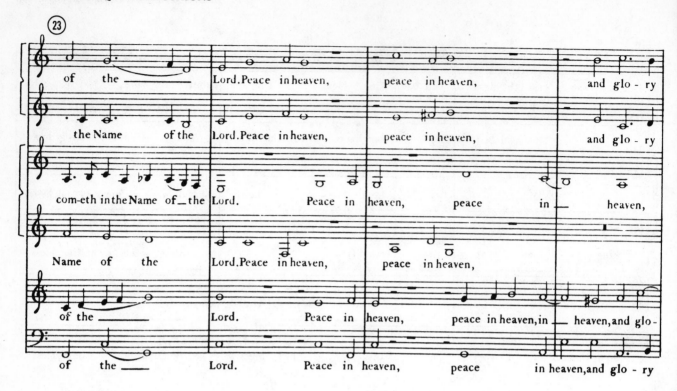

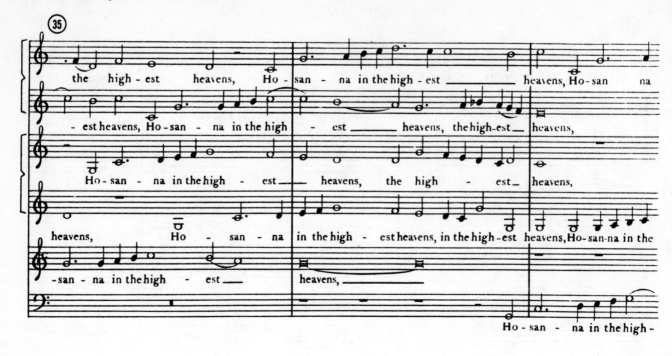

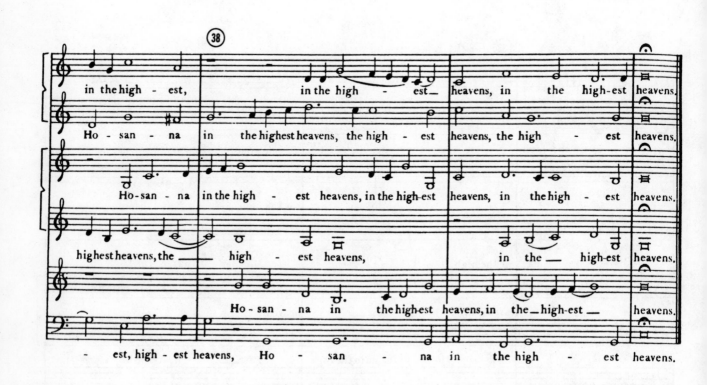

PART TWO

Late Baroque Compositions

Since this anthology concentrates on the repertory most emphasized in theory and analysis courses, Baroque music is represented chiefly by works of J.S. Bach. Part Two requires little prefatory comment beyond a summary of its genres and forms.

Examples of genres based on imitative counterpoint include two inventions, six fugues, and four canons of Bach, as well as a fugue of Handel and a *Preludio* from a Corelli trio sonata. Two of the Bach chorale preludes and the Corelli *Allemanda* also feature imitation prominently.

Four pieces are constructed over a ground. The Handel keyboard *chaconne*, besides being in the form of sectional variations, is a useful model for students of elementary harmony; the Bach *chaconne* for violin solo is a challenge for more advanced students. *Dido's Lament* of Purcell and the *Crucifixus* of Bach are included both for their use of ground bass and for their rich and varied chromaticism.

The binary form with both parts repeated is represented by the pieces from the Anna Magdalena Notebook, various suite movements, and the Scarlatti sonata. In choosing these, a general consideration was to show the form worked out in a wide variety of ways—with different kinds of harmonic and melodic design. All of these examples, together with related ones in other parts of the book, are listed under "Binary forms" in the General Index.

A group of *cantus firmus* compositions comprises three chorale preludes of Bach and the excerpt from his chorale variations, *O Gott, du frommer Gott*. The four pieces from *The Musical Offering* will be of interest primarily as canons, but they are also "variations" on a short cantus firmus that appears in its simplest form in Canon 2.

The principle of alternation is the formal basis of the Couperin *rondeau* and the movement from Bach's second Brandenburg concerto, with its *ritornello* form. Handel's aria, "Father of Heaven," also makes conspicuous use of *ritornello*.

Part Two also contains several preludes or prelude-like first movements that reveal no conventional form: the two preludes from the *Well-tempered Clavier*, the Corelli *Preludio*, and the *Adagio* from the Handel violin sonata.

Other features of this part include several pieces with figured bass (each with a staff provided for the realization), and score-reading problems of increasing size, the largest being the Brandenburg concerto movement (see "Figured bass" and "Score" in the Index). The Bach canons, once solved and written out, are useful for practice in musicianship: The student sings one line while playing the other(s) at the keyboard.

Additional examples of Baroque music are given in the Appendix (page 593), which comprises harmonizations of 27 chorale melodies. Though most are by Bach, six date from the early seventeenth century.

Two Movements

from *Sonate da camera a tre,* Op. 4

(publ. 1694)

Arcangelo Corelli

(1653–1713)

Corelli's Opus 4 is a collection of trio sonatas. These two excerpts show the kind of texture (two high parts with continuo) typical not only of the trio sonata, but frequently found in other genres of Baroque music. The first, from the fifth sonata of the collection, exhibits simple sequences and modulations. Perception of the harmonies will require some reduction of the elaborate bass part. (For other examples of elaborate bass under simpler upper parts, see pages 94, 373, and 606.) The second excerpt, being an opening movement, ends (typically) with a Phrygian cadence (i.e., IV⁶—V). How are its phrases articulated? What is the form? What older genres employ a similar procedure?

One very practical way to begin analysis of these movements is through realization of the figured bass. An extra staff is provided for this purpose.

Allemanda (from Sonata No. 5)

Preludio (from Sonata No. 8)

Grave

Violino I

Violino II

Dido's Lament

from *Dido and Aeneas* (in vocal score)

(1689)

Henry Purcell

(ca. 1659–1695)

Text: Nahum Tate

The grieving Dido, abandoned by her lover Aeneas, bids farewell to her lady-in-waiting, Belinda. In this aria the composer employs a form of the chromatic ground often used in Baroque music to portray death. Here the ground is five bars long. How do the phrases of the vocal part compare in length? Where do cadences occur? What is the form of the aria?

Comparison may be made with Bach's *Crucifixus* from the B minor mass (page 151) and the chaconnes of Handel and Bach (pages 94 and 114).

Dido and Aeneas by Henry Purcell, Edward J. Dent, ed. Copyright, 1925, by the Oxford University Press, London. Renewed in U. S. A. 1953. Reprinted by permission.

vades me, Death__ is now__ a wel - come guest.

Strings

When I am laid,__ am laid _____ in

earth, may my wrongs__ cre - ate no trou - ble, no trou-ble in__ thy

breast. When I am laid,__ am laid _____ in earth, may my

wrongs ___ cre - ate no trou - ble, no trou - ble in___ thy breast.

Re - mem - ber me, Re - mem - ber me, But

ah! _____ for-get my fate, Re-mem-ber me, but ah! _____

for - get my_ fate! Re-mem-ber me, Re-mem-ber me, But

ah! _____ for-get my fate, Re-mem-ber me, but ah! _____

for - get my___ fate!

La Bandoline

from *Pièces de Clavecin*, Fifth Ordre
(publ. 1713)

François Couperin
(1668–1733)

This elegant piece may have been named after a woman from Bandol. All the words and ornaments in the score are Couperin's. The ornaments may generally be interpreted as follows:[1]

pincé   tremblement

An example of the Baroque rondeau, *La Bandoline* may be compared with examples of the rondo by later composers.

Rondeau

Légérement, sans vitesse

La main droite coulée;
Et la gauche marquée.

Copyright 1932 by Louise B. M. Dyer. Reprinted by permission of Editions de l'Oiseau-Lyre, Monaco, from *Oeuvres Complètes de Francois Couperin* (Cauchie), Vol. 2, pp. 141–143.

[1]See Frederick Neumann's article, "Misconceptions about the French Trill in the Seventeenth and Eighteenth Centuries," in *The Musical Quarterly*, April 1964, pp. 188–206.

1er Couplet

Rondeau

2^e Couplet

Rondeau

3ᵉ Couplet

Rondeau

Four Pieces

from the *Notebook for Anna Magdalena Bach (1725)*

Anonymous

It has been conjectured that the *Notebook* of 1725 began as a birthday gift from J. S. Bach to his young second wife. Be that as it may, it grew during the ensuing years into a collection of music of the Bach household, the pieces copied in from time to time by various members thereof. While the music of Bach himself is well represented in the collection, pieces by other composers, known and unknown, were also included. Several have been attributed to the young Karl Philipp Emanuel.

The four simple pieces given here all have a double bar in the middle. In what ways do they differ in form? Analyze their harmony, particularly where they are composed of only two voices.

March

What is the explanation of the major ninth on the second quarter of bar 1? What is the essential voice-leading underlying the sequences? Where are the strongest cadences?

Minuet

Aria

In the *Notebook* this aria is provided with text—a six-stanza poem entitled "Edifying Thoughts of a Tobacco Smoker." It is possible J. S. Bach was the poem's author. An excellent English rendering of it is given in *The Bach Reader*, H. David and A. Mendel, eds., Norton, 1945, p. 97.

So oft ich mei - ne To - backs - Pfei - fe, mit gu - tem
Zeit - ver - treib er - grei - fe, so gibt sie

Kna - ster an - ge - füllt, zur Lust und
mir ein Trauer -

1. zur Lust und

2. bild

und fü - get   die - se   Leh - re   bei,

dass ich der - sel - ben   ähn - lich sei.   sei.

Polonaise

Adagio

from *Sonata in F major for Violin and Continuo*, Op. 1, No. 12
(publ. ca. 1724)

George Frideric Handel
(1685–1759)

This movement, the first of a four-movement work, is not in a conventional form. Prelude-like in character, it sets the stage for the subsequent movements, all of which are in typical binary form with a double bar in the middle. Of course, the piece has a form of its own that should not be missed. Also, study of the piece is not complete until the figured bass is realized. It can be written out or, with practice, played directly from the figures.

Chaconne

from *Trois Leçons*

(publ. 1733)

George Frideric Handel

(1685–1759)

> This chaconne is simpler than the monumental example given on page 114, and we recommend studying it first. Discover what elements remain constant throughout the piece, then pinpoint the unique attribute(s) of each variation.
>
> A composition such as this cannot rely simply on variation technique for its success, but must also convince as a single large form. Draw a diagram representing the large shape created by the entire series of variations.

Fugue in B flat major

from *Six Fugues*

(ca. 1720?–publ. 1735)

George Frideric Handel

(1685–1759)

Comparison of this composition with the keyboard fugues of Bach will immediately reveal many differences in procedure. (Notice, for example, the matter of the number of voices.) Such differences should not be viewed as "rule-breaking," but simply as characteristic of Handel's conception of the genre.

Recitative:
"Thy Rebuke Hath Broken his Heart"

No. 27 from *The Messiah*

(1741)

George Frideric Handel

(1685–1759)

Text based on Psalms *69: 20 (King James version)*

This tenor recitative falls between a chorus in C minor, "He trusted in God," and a tenor arioso in E minor, "Behold, and see." It is a particularly effective series of chromatic modulations. Sing the vocal line while playing your realization of the figured bass. (An extra staff is provided for the realization.) How is each modulation accomplished? Which one employs the most radical use of chromaticism?

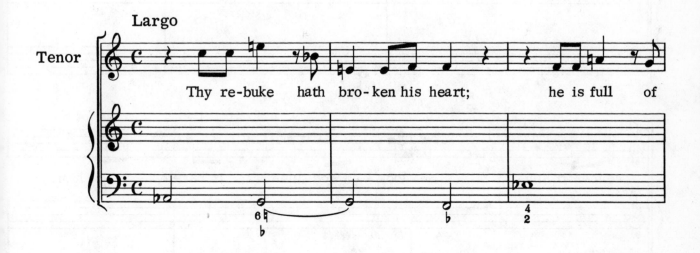

"Father of Heaven"

from *Judas Maccabaeus*
(1746)

George Frideric Handel
(1685–1759)

Text: Thomas Morell

The First Book of Maccabees, with its account of the victory of the Israelites over the army of Antiochus, provided the basis of the libretto of Handel's oratorio *Judas Maccabaeus*. (The libretto was also intended as a compliment to the Duke of Cumberland upon his victory over the army of the Scots.) In keeping with the military theme, this work has much loud and fast music, but Act III begins on a note of calm with the aria given here, in which an Israelite priest invokes God's blessing on the Festival of Lights.

"Father of Heaven" observes all the conventions of the late Baroque *aria da capo* except one: The *da capo* is written out. Compare carefully the two outer sections. Also discover the ways in which the middle section is differentiated from the outer ones. Another aspect well worth study is the contribution of the three upper string parts to the design of the whole. (As was his custom when composing large concerted works, Handel here did not bother to write out complete figures for the keyboard player.)

nize _____ the feast of lights.

Gavottes I and II

from *English Suite No. 3 in G minor*, BWV 808

(before 1722)

Johann Sebastian Bach

(1685–1750)

Analysis of the basic motive, the phrases, and the overall form are obvious first steps. Deeper study of the harmony and voice leading of *Gavotte I* will reveal that, although the piece has only two parts—treble and bass—it often has three or four implied *voices*. (A simpler example of this phenomenon will be found on page 157.) In *Gavotte II*, what harmonies do you hear besides that of the obvious tonic pedal? What is the harmony in bar 46, first half?

Gavotte II
(ou la Musette)

(Gavotte I. d. c.)

Sarabande

from *Partita No. 1 in B flat major*, BWV 825

(publ. 1726)

Johann Sebastian Bach

(1685–1750)

A very practical analysis problem is presented by the ornate melodic line of this sarabande: How is one to articulate and phrase it? At first the ornateness would seem to obscure the essential continuity of the line, but close examination by means of the process of reduction will reveal many long-range stepwise connections that give direction and meaning to the elaborate figuration. Making such a melodic reduction will be somewhat similar to perceiving the *cantus firmus* in a highly ornamented chorale prelude such as *Wenn wir in höchsten Noten sein* (page 159). While the sarabande has, of course, no *cantus firmus*, it clearly has "main," or "high-ranking," tones around which tones of subordinate rank cluster. (Note: In bar 5, the E flat against E natural is correct.)

Minuets I and II

from *Suite No. 1 in G major for Violoncello Solo,* BWV 1007

(ca. 1720)

Johann Sebastian Bach

(1685–1750)

Bach was a master at constructing melodic lines that consist of both a top voice and its bass—and sometimes inner voices as well. These two minuets are relatively simple examples of such "compound," or "polyphonic," melodic lines. In such a line, it is sometimes inevitable that one or more notes of a voice—especially a bass voice—will have to be omitted, but careful listening will usually reveal what is implied. (A tricky spot is bars 4 through 8. What is the implied bass here?) We recommend starting with *Minuet II,* the simpler and more explicit example. Compound melodic line is also prominent in the pieces on pages 108, 110, 114, and 157.

Menuet I.

Menuet II.

Chaconne

from *Partita No. 2 in D minor for Violin Solo*, BWV 1004

(ca. 1720)

Johann Sebastian Bach

(1685–1750)

This work, the fifth and last movement of a suite, is the most celebrated of Baroque chaconnes. Its composer, restricting himself to quite conventional procedures, has built, within a pitch gamut of only three octaves, a monumental musical edifice as rich in variety as in elements that unify. What holds together this enormous piece? And as it continues, what factors create divisions, both small and large? A simpler chaconne is given on page 94. See also the pieces on pages 76 and 151.

Two Inventions
(1720–1723)

Johann Sebastian Bach
(1685–1750)

Most of Bach's "two-part" inventions are based on either a short motivic subject that usually is first stated alone, or a long subject composed of two simultaneous parts that are invertible at the octave. An example of each of these two types is given here. In the B minor invention, how do the first two bars of the left-hand part relate to the rest of the piece?

Invention 1 in C major, BWV 772

Invention 15 in B minor, BWV 786

Preludes and Fugues

from *The Well-tempered Clavier, Book I*

(1722)

Johann Sebastian Bach

(1685–1750)

Bach's great cycle of preludes and fugues in all major and minor keys reveals as much variety of expression as any set of character pieces from the Romantic era. While our selection attempts to give a glimpse of this remarkable variety, it aims, most of all, to provide examples of the chief types of fugue and fugal technique. One might begin with the noble, pensive fugue in G minor (page 135) since it displays many "standard" characteristics. (Fugues by other composers and from other periods will be found on pages 98, 264, 517, and 544; a fugal section appears, as well, on page 188 at bar 189.)

Prelude and Fugue 1 in C major, BWV 846[2]

[2]An analysis by Heinrich Schenker of the prelude appears in his *Five Graphic Music Analyses*, ed. by Felix Salzer (New York: Dover Publications, 1969), pp. 36–37.

Fugue 2 in C minor, BWV 847

Fugue 5 in D major, BWV 850

Of the six Bach fugues in this book, this one is farthest from the traditional academic notion of what a proper fugue should be. In what ways does it conspicuously differ from the others in general lay-out and style?

Fugue 8 in D sharp minor, BWV 853

What is the nature of a subject that lends itself most readily to a variety of fugal devices? Notice that many of the statements of the subject of this fugue differ from the opening statement in one or more melodic intervals. What causes this? Comment on the absence of a countersubject in this fugue.

Fugue 13 in F sharp major, BWV 858

Fugue 16 in G minor, BWV 861

Prelude 22 in B flat minor, BMV 867

While this slow, intensely expressive prelude is an example *par excellence* of monomotivic composition, it must, like any composition, be conceived not only as a *unit*, but also as a *unit with articulated portions*. Consider, then, not only how it is built of a single motive, and how it projects a single large shape, but also the nature of its phrases and parts. In modern performance of Baroque music, the questions of instrumentation and dynamics are often subjects of controversy. But in the performance of this prelude—regardless of what keyboard instrument it is played on—how do the notes themselves achieve a measure of dynamic gradation and contrast? (For somewhat similar compositions from another period, see the Chopin prelude and etude on pages 370 and 388.)

Four Canons
from *The Musical Offering*, BWV 1079
(1747)

Johann Sebastian Bach
(1685–1750)

The term *canon* comes from the Greek word for rule or law. In musical parlance it denotes a type of composition in which a leading voice, or *dux*, is strictly imitated by a following voice, the *comes*, or by more than one follower. The rule denotes the time and pitch intervals at which the follower enters, and the form it is to take—whether an exact replica of the leader, or inverted, augmented, and so on. Of the many types of canon, the simplest is perhaps the round. Exactly what is the rule governing the performance of "Three Blind Mice"?

The canons below are based on a theme purportedly given to Bach by King Frederick the Great as a subject for improvisation. Bach later sent the king a "musical offering" in which the same royal theme served as the basis of an impressive collection of pieces, many of them canons. In the notation of some of these, Bach carried on the old tradition of the *riddle canon:* The canon is written as one part only, and the reader is left to figure out how it is to be performed.

It is important to distinguish between the rule, which merely indicates how to perform the canon, and the way the canon operates within the triadic tonal system. (What harmonic principle governs the construction of "Three Blind Mice"?) To discover their rules is only one reason—and a superficial one—for the inclusion of these canons here. The real analytic problem is to discover how they are composed. (For other examples, see "Canons" in the General Index.[3]

1

How would one go about composing a canon of this type?

Canon a 2

³Solutions to all the *Musical Offering*'s canons by Bach's pupil, Johann Philipp Kirnberger (1721-1783), are given in Volume 31 of the *Gesellschaft* edition of Bach's works.

2

Here a two-voice canon is set over a third, non-canonic, line—the king's theme.

3

The upside-down clef signifies that the *comes* is to be inverted, but there is no indication of where it is to enter. Instead, Bach gives the Latin for "Seek and ye shall find."

When inversion occurs in tonal music, it is nearly always *tonal*. This example of inversion is particularly arresting in that it is *real* throughout, that is, it requires not a single alteration in interval size. What particular characteristics of his material does Bach exploit to achieve this *tour de force*? What is the axis of symmetry in this canon? (Twentieth-century examples of symmetrical organization around an axis are given on pages 508, 512, and 513.)

4

This amusing example bears the clue, "In whole steps." As in No. 2, the king's theme is played against a canonic duet. The clefs indicate which of the two notated parts is to be performed canonically and at what interval. On reaching the repeat marks, all parts start again—but what has happened?

Canon a 2. Per tonos. [Ascendente modulatione ascendat Gloria Regis]

Brandenburg Concerto No. 2

BWV 1047, first movement

(1721)

Johann Sebastian Bach

(1685–1750)

The development of the Baroque concerto grosso culminated in the masterpieces of Handel's Opus 6 and Bach's six "Brandenburg" concertos. While the famous movement given here, first, vividly features the contrast between concertino and ripieno, and, second, makes prominent use of ritornelli, it is not true that all fast movements of concerti grossi do so to the same extent, for there is no "concerto grosso form" (in the sense of "sonata form"), and the variety of procedure in the repertoire as a whole is enormous.

To explore this movement, one might start by isolating the various melodic materials and relating them to ripieno and concertino. Are some melodies confined to just the ripieno or the concertino? In which various ways—besides simply pitting concertino against ripieno—is contrast of sound or texture achieved? How is the complex mosaic of contrasting materials related to the over-all tonal plan? (Study of this movement could be aided by making a large diagram.)

The top four lines of the score constitute the concertino, the next four the ripieno. (Note that *violone* is the double bass and sounds an octave lower than written.) The bottom line is that of the continuo, which accompanies throughout. The only transposing instrument is the trumpet, which sounds a perfect 4th higher than written. The flauto is the recorder, not the transverse flute.

In this book the ritornello principle is further illustrated by the Handel aria on page 103. Also the concertino-vs.-ripieno idea was carried on in the Classical solo concerto. Consider the Mozart concerto movement on page 237 from this point of view.

Score begins on page 144.

Tromba.

Flauto.
(Flür à bec)

Oboe.

Violino.

Violino I.
di ripieno.

Violino II.
di ripieno.

Viola
di ripieno.

Violone
di ripieno.

Violoncello
e Cembalo
all'unisono.

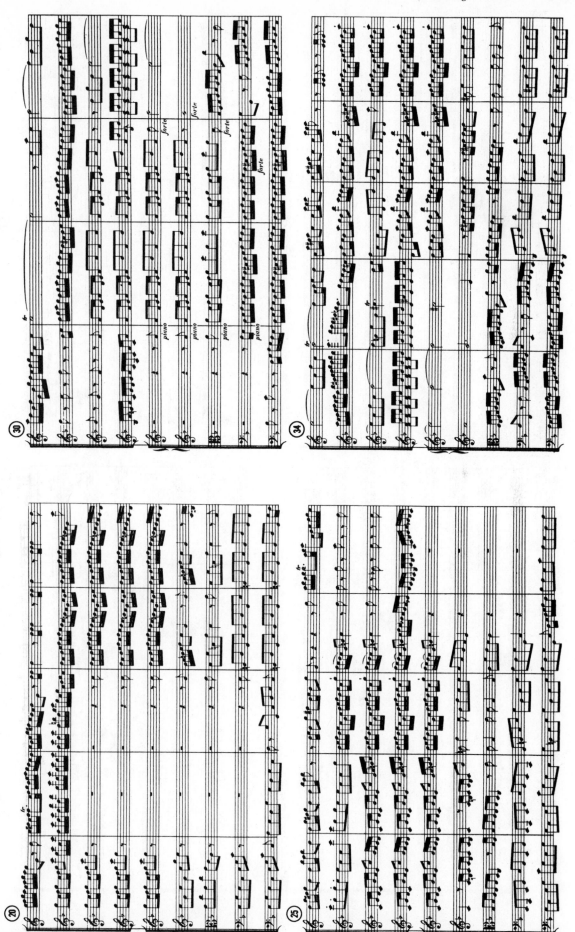

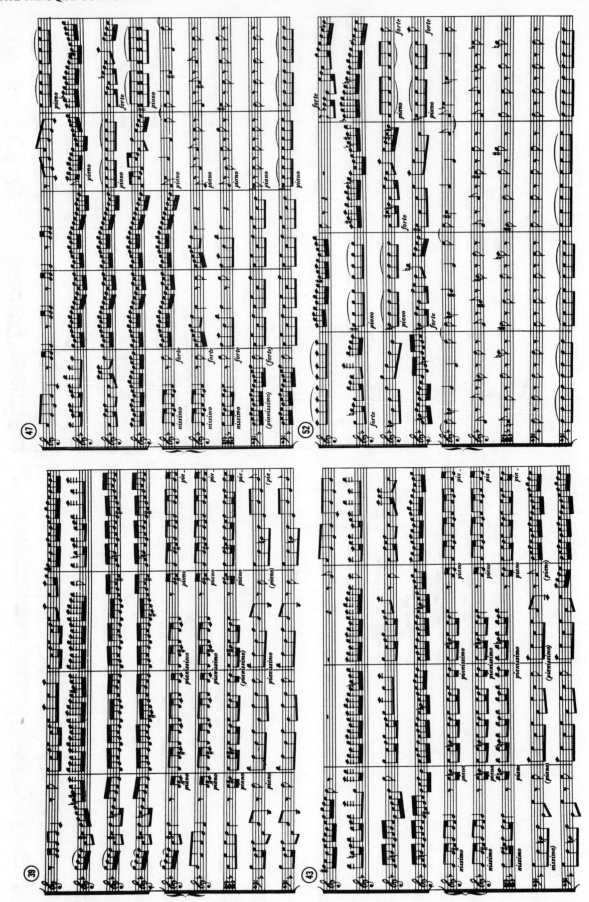

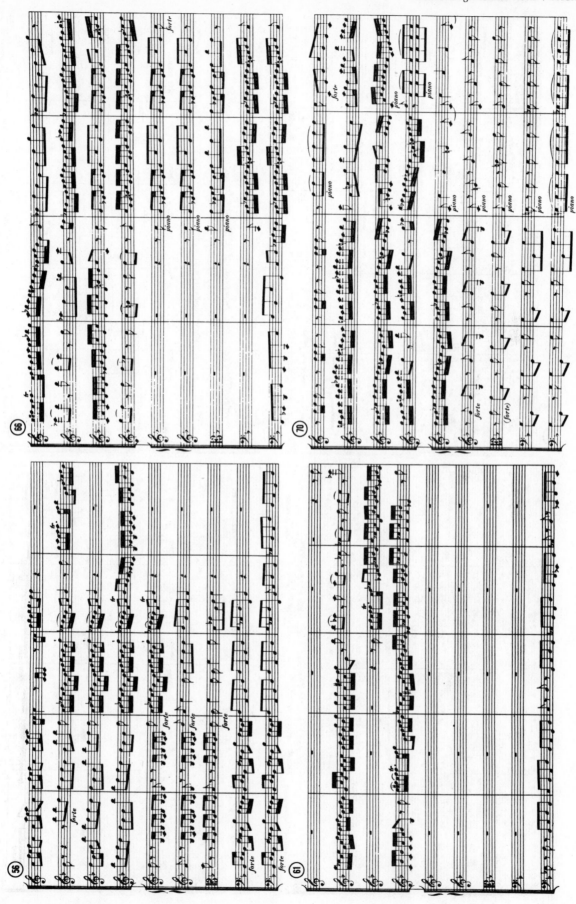

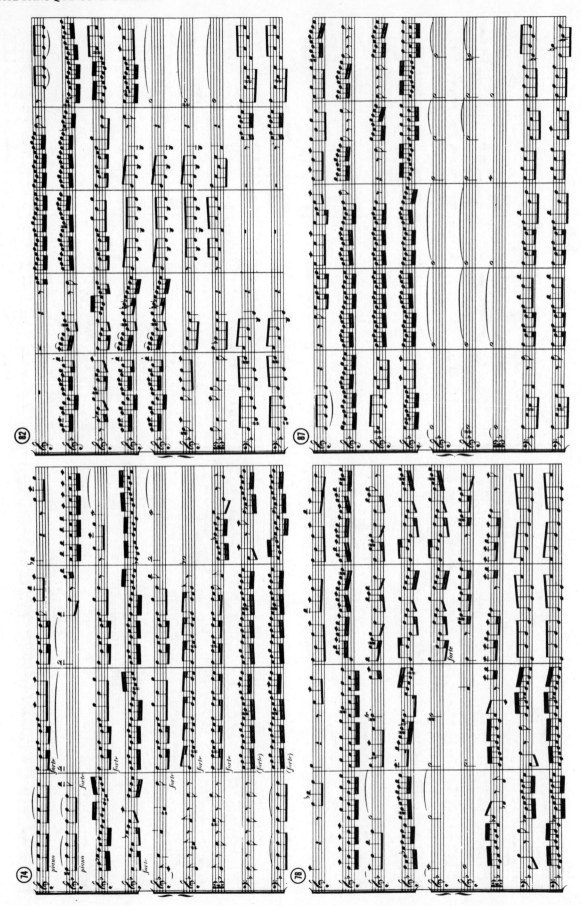

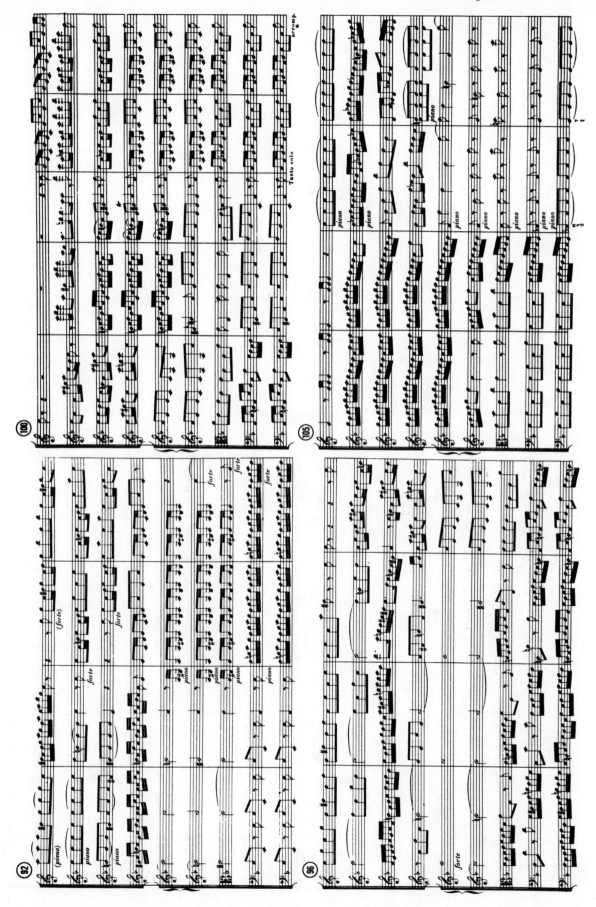

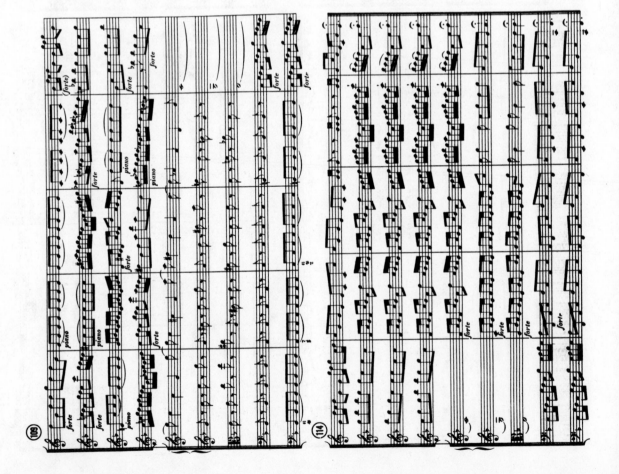

Crucifixus

from *Mass in B minor*, BWV 232

(1733)

Johann Sebastian Bach

(1685–1750)

It is clear that the ground of this affecting passacaglia descends from the root of the tonic chord to the root of the dominant, but how is one to account for the intervening motion, particularly the abundant chromaticism, beyond merely labeling each vertical sonority? The ground is four bars long. Do the upper parts consistently form four-bar phrases parallel with the ground? What factors create the work's several large sections? How do the final five bars relate to the rest of this movement?

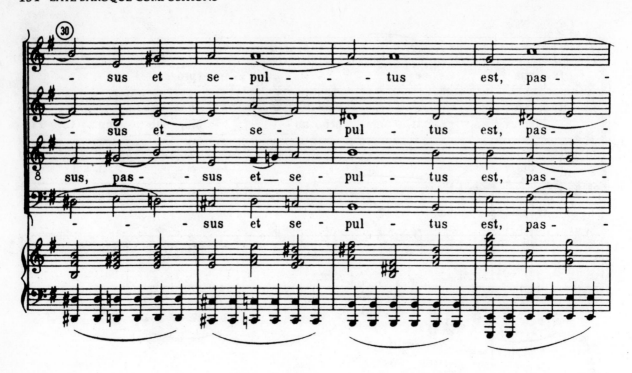

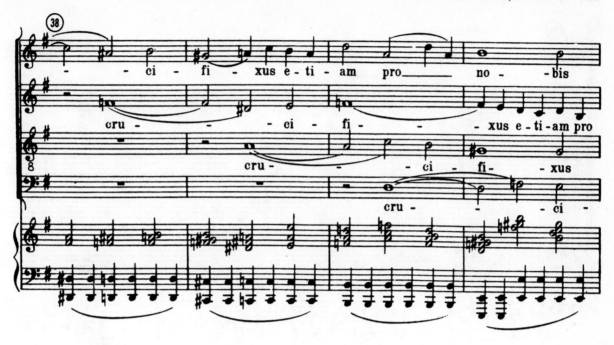

O Gott, du frommer Gott

BWV 767

(ca. 1700)

Johann Sebastian Bach

(1685–1750)

This is the fourth in a set of nine organ variations, or *partitas*, on the chorale *O Gott du frommer Gott*, which begins as follows:

O   Gott   du   from-mer   Gott,   du   Brunn-quell   gu – ter   Ga – ben

The problem is to trace the *several* voices inherent in the right-hand part. (Other problems of this kind will be found on pages 108, 110, and 114.) The tempo of this partita, though not indicated, should be fairly fast.

Three Chorale Preludes

Johann Sebastian Bach
(1685–1750)

The chorale prelude is an organ composition based on a chorale and performed in the Lutheran service prior to the singing of the chorale by the congregation. Three of the many types of prelude are illustrated here. The first two are from the *Orgelbüchlein* (Little Organ Book), an unfinished collection of preludes, in which Bach planned to provide for every occasion of the church year. Both the second and third examples are based on the same chorale.

Jesu, meine Freude, BWV 610
(ca. 1717)

Discover the basic harmonization that underlies the elaboration. Is it the same as that of the setting of the chorale on page 610?

Wenn wir in höchsten Nöten sein, BWV 641

(ca. 1717)

The hearer of *When We Are in Direst Need* cannot fully appreciate it without knowing the chorale in its original form. If you do not know it, try to find it beneath the luxurious embellishment. The quarter-note pulse should be taken quite slowly.

Vor deinen Tron tret' ich hiermit, BWV 668

from Eighteen Chorale Preludes

(1750)

Bach's last composition, dictated on his deathbed, is an organ prelude based on the chorale *Wenn wir in höchsten Nöten sein*. Taking a line from an inner stanza of that hymn, Bach titled this work "Before Thy Throne I Now Appear."

The chorale, with very little adornment, lies in the upper part. How is it motivically related to the lower parts? Also, compare the lower parts with those of the previous chorale prelude.

Chorale

Sonata in E major

K. 380 (Longo 23)

(1754?)

Domenico Scarlatti

(1685–1757)

We offer this justly well-known sonata as typical of the way in which Scarlatti frequently handled some of the more general aspects of binary form. Compare it with other examples of binary form in this book? What does it have in common with the sonata form of the late eighteenth century? Notice that the dominant chord opens and closes the section bounded by bars 41 and 57. What happens between these points? Explain each tone in bar 15.

PART THREE

Classical Compositions

This part of the anthology emphasizes the musical forms of the high Classic era. Chief of these is sonata form, of which there are seven examples from piano sonatas, three from string quartets, and one from a piano concerto. All these are cited under "Sonata form" in the General Index (which also lists two related examples—one each from the 19th and 20th centuries). Each was selected to show a different way of working out the form. Study might begin with the Clementi F major movement and continue with the first movement of Beethoven's F minor sonata, Op. 2, No. 1, or of Mozart's K. 333. (The latter work is given complete.)

Part Three also contains three rondos (see Part Two for a Couperin rondeau), as well as examples of sonata form without development, compound ternary form, theme with variations, fantasia, and fugue. These examples, plus similar ones from other historical periods, are likewise listed in the index, as are examples of various *small* forms—particularly "rounded" binary—that are imbedded in the large ones. Attention is also called to the sequence of examples listed under "Minuets and scherzos" in the index.

Nine examples in this part are given in score: two symphony movements and one string quartet movement of Haydn, the concerto movement of Mozart (and the excerpt from his *Requiem*, which is in vocal score), and the string quartet, Op. 135, of Beethoven, which is given complete.

In analyzing a particular piece of music, it is important to distinguish between its similarity to other pieces and that which makes it unique. Every sonata form, for example, has an exposition, a development section, and a recapitulation. But a sonata of Mozart or Beethoven has endured because, in addition to its expected traditional characteristics, it is supremely *unlike* any other. The ability to perceive the nature of a great work's originality testifies to a high degree of musical insight.

Piano Sonata in E flat major

HOB. XVI/52, first movement

(1794)

Joseph Haydn

(1732–1809)

One of Haydn's last piano sonatas, this work embodies a youthful inventiveness in a ripened language only age can command.

The nature of the second theme and of the closing theme, the abrupt modulation at bar 68 and its place in the tonal plan of the movement, and the chord background of bars 109 and 110 are a few of the many details that deserve close investigation.[1]

[1]Heinrich Schenker analyzes this sonata in the third issue of *Der Tonwille* (Vienna: A. Gutmann Verlag, 1922; republished by Universal Edition). Of particular interest is his bar-by-bar reduction showing both the basic rhythm of each bar and the basic voice-leading.

Symphony No. 101 in D major
Third and Fourth Movements
(1794)

Joseph Haydn
(1732–1809)

Haydn's "Clock" symphony, which owes its nickname to the opening rhythm of the second movement, is one of twelve symphonies written in London between 1791 and 1795 for concerts produced by Johann Salomon.

The third movement is a typical symphonic minuet and trio. It may be compared with the other minuets and, particularly, with the scherzos in this book. The fourth movement, though in a form rather usual for final movements of Classical works, contains a number of surprises.

Third Movement

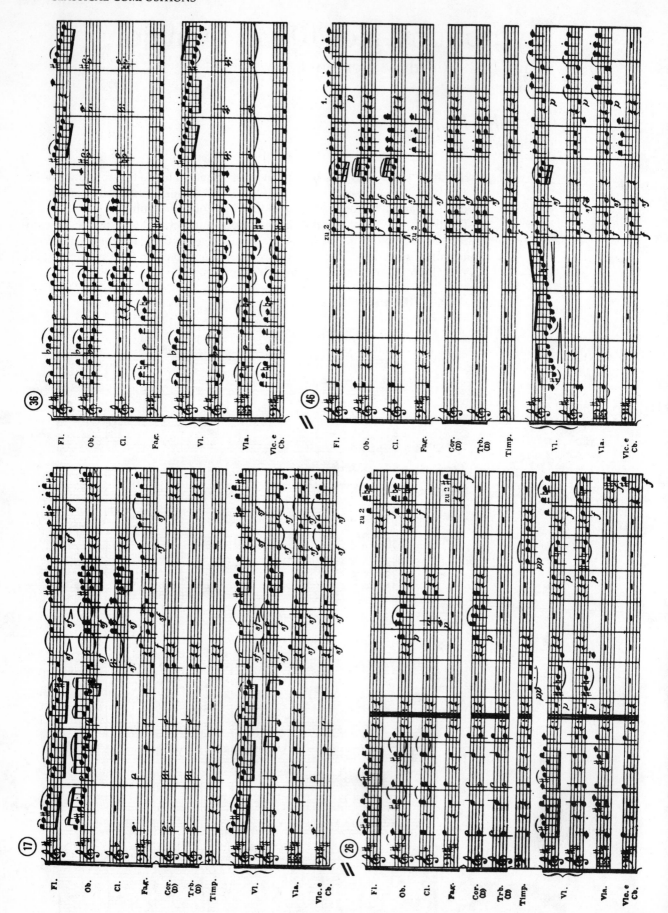

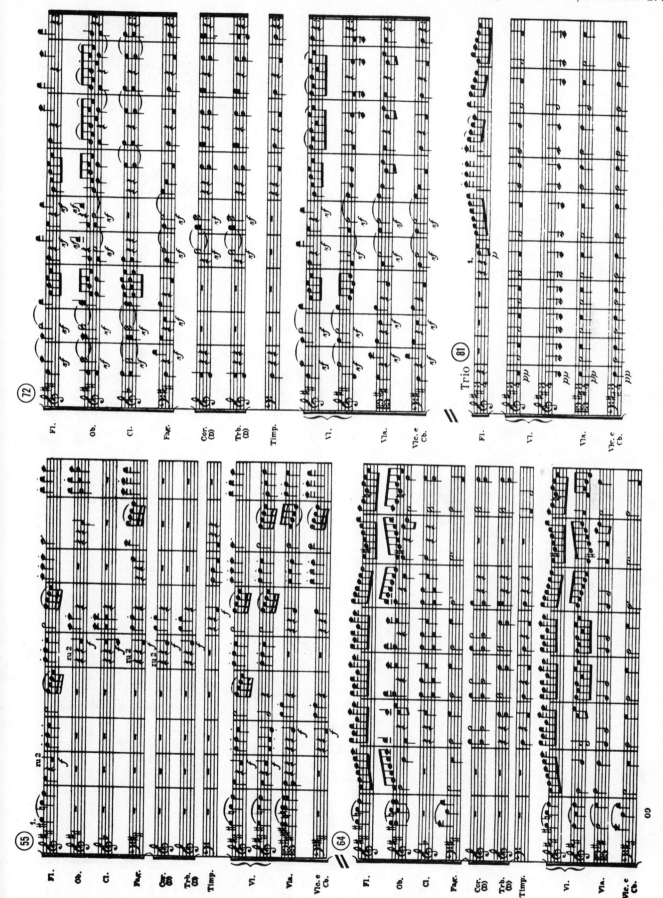

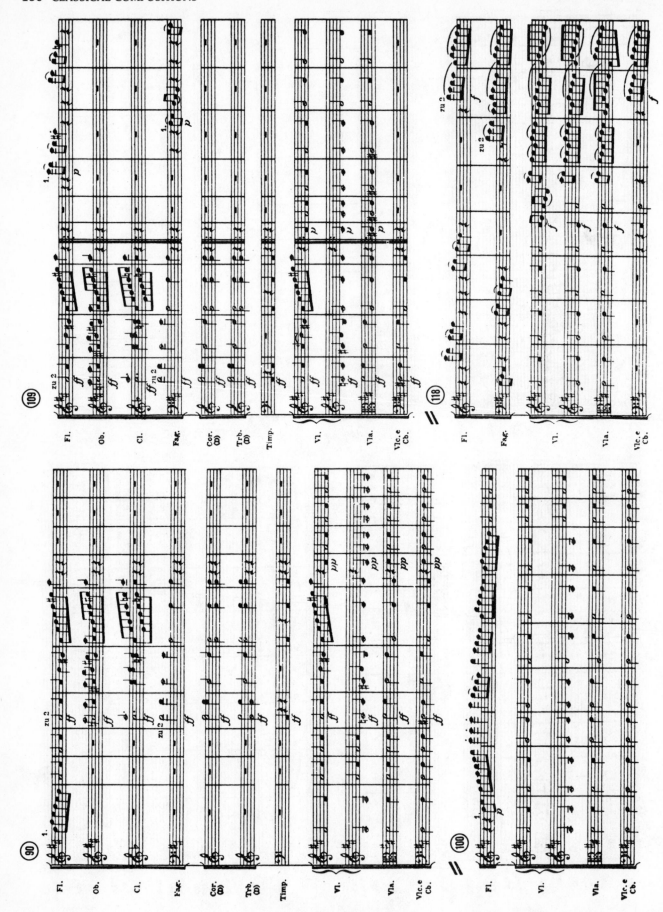

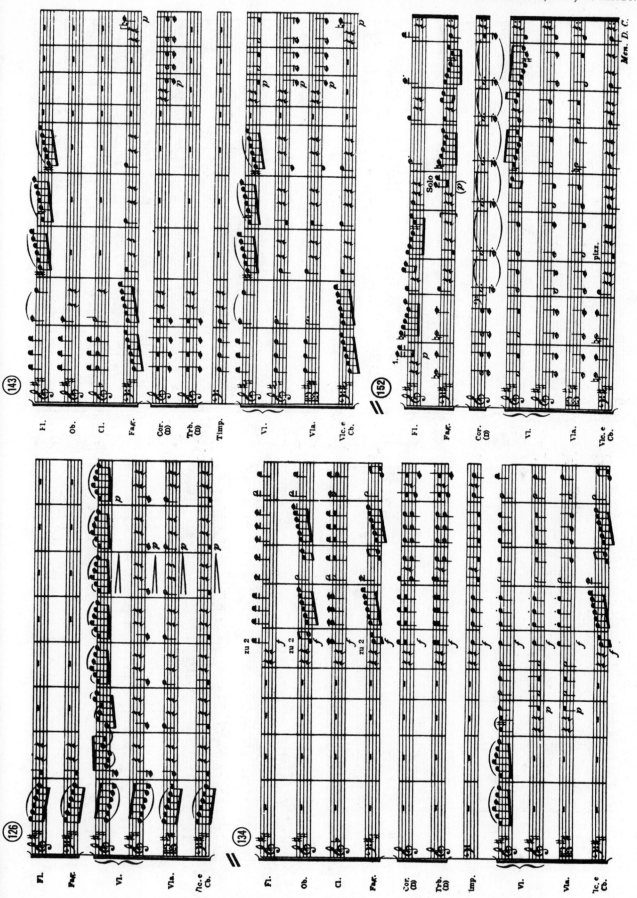

Fourth Movement

Finale. Vivace.

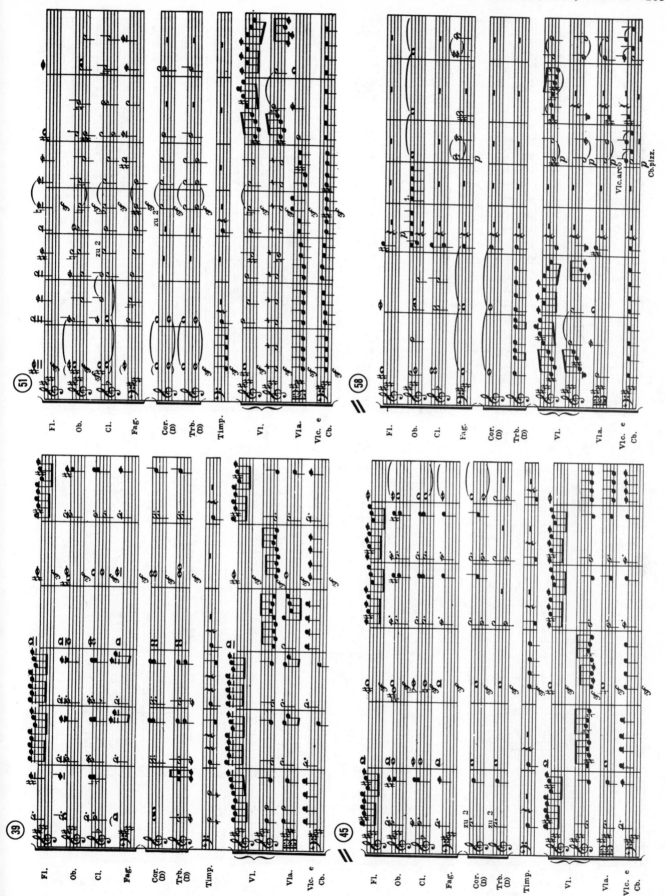

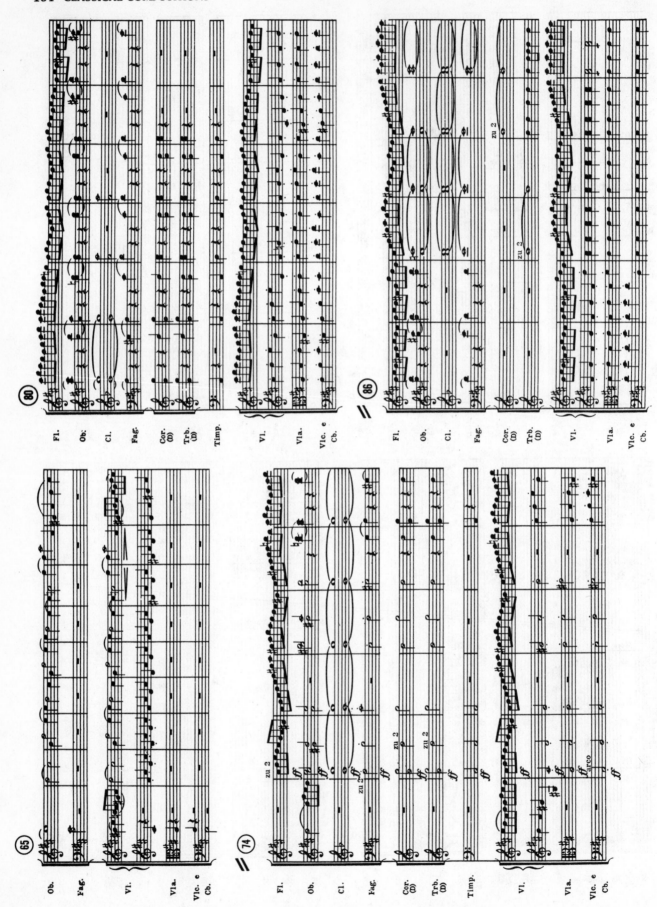

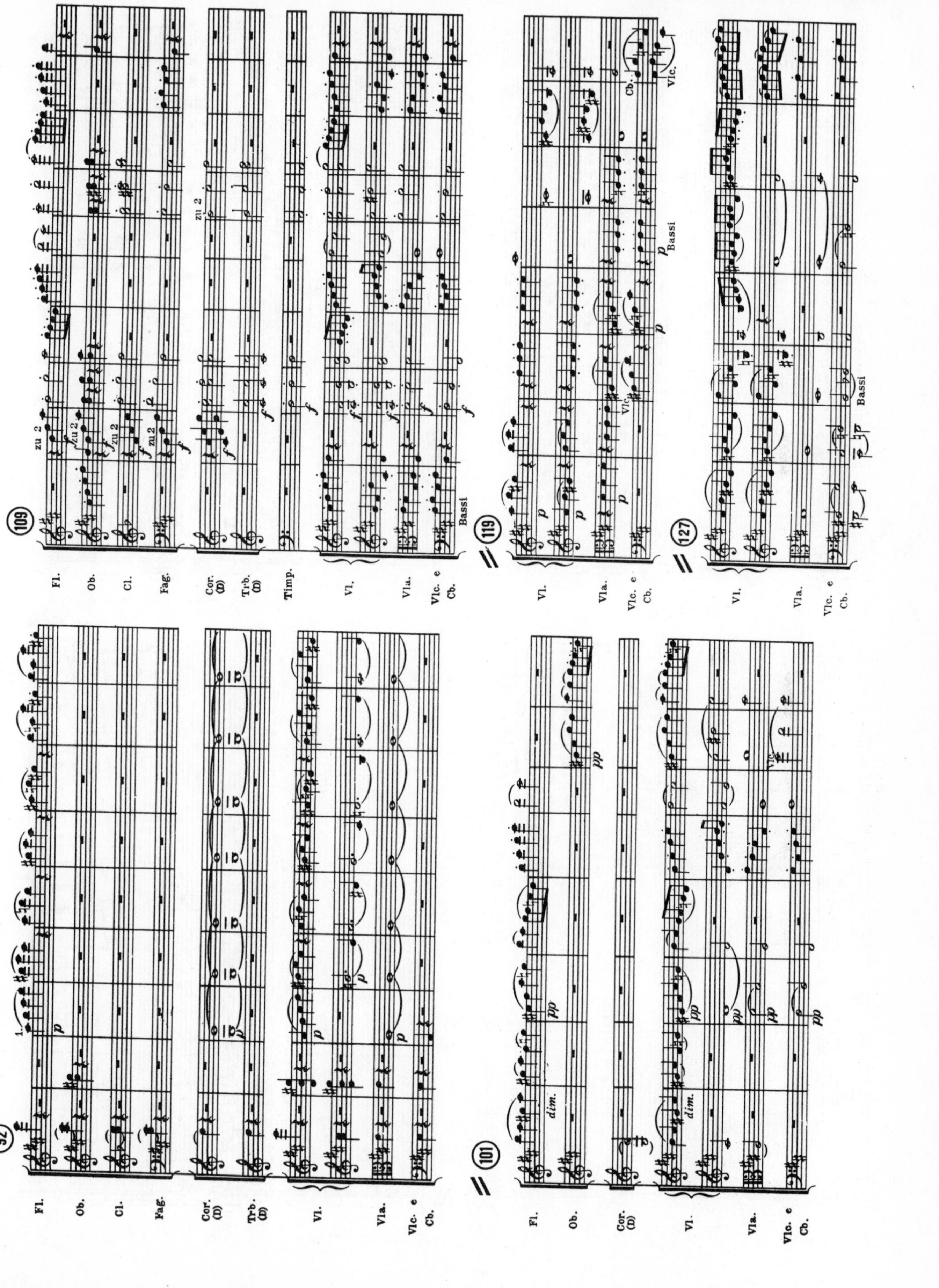

92
Fl.
Ob.
Cl.
Fag.
Cor. (D)
Trb. (D)
Vl.
Vla.
Vlc. e Cb.
101
Fl.
Ob.
Cor. (D)
Vl.
Vla.
Vlc. e Cb.
dim.
Vlc.
109
Fl.
Ob.
Cl.
Fag.
Cor. (D)
Trb. (D)
Timp.
Vl.
Vla.
Vlc. e Cb.
zu 2
Bassi
119
Vl.
Vla.
Vlc. e Cb.
Vlc.
Cb.
Bassi
127
Vl.
Vla.
Vlc. e Cb.
Bassi

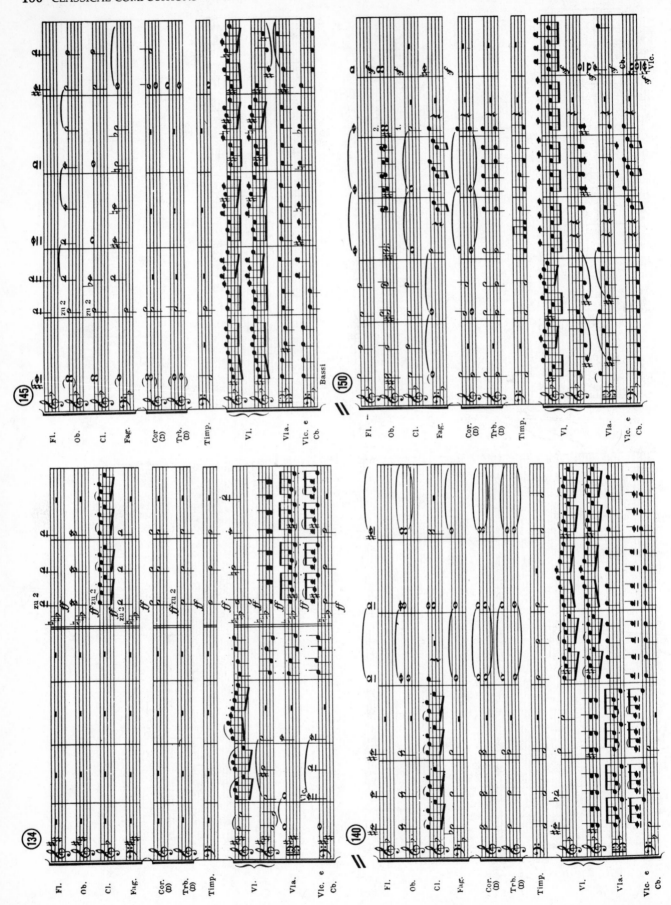

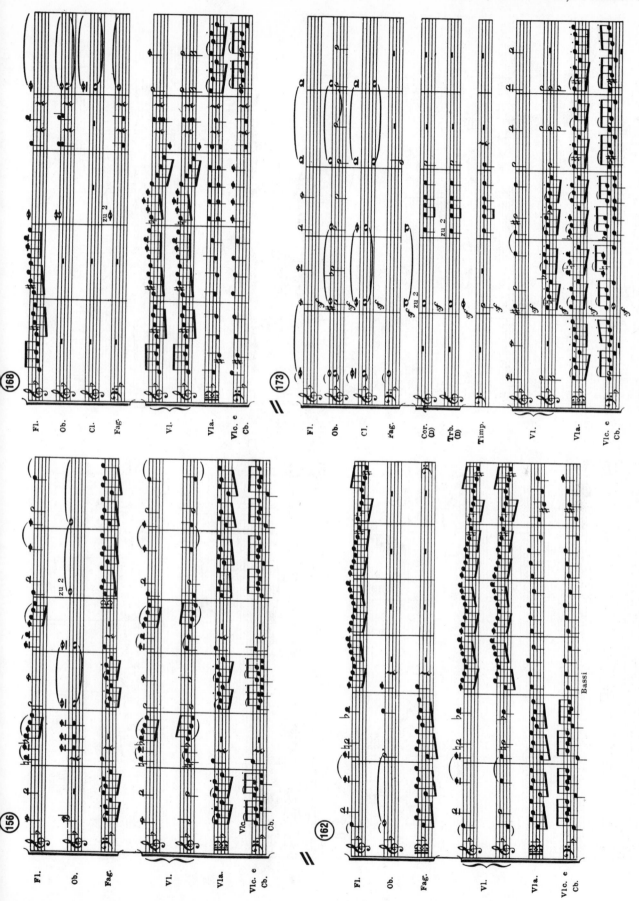

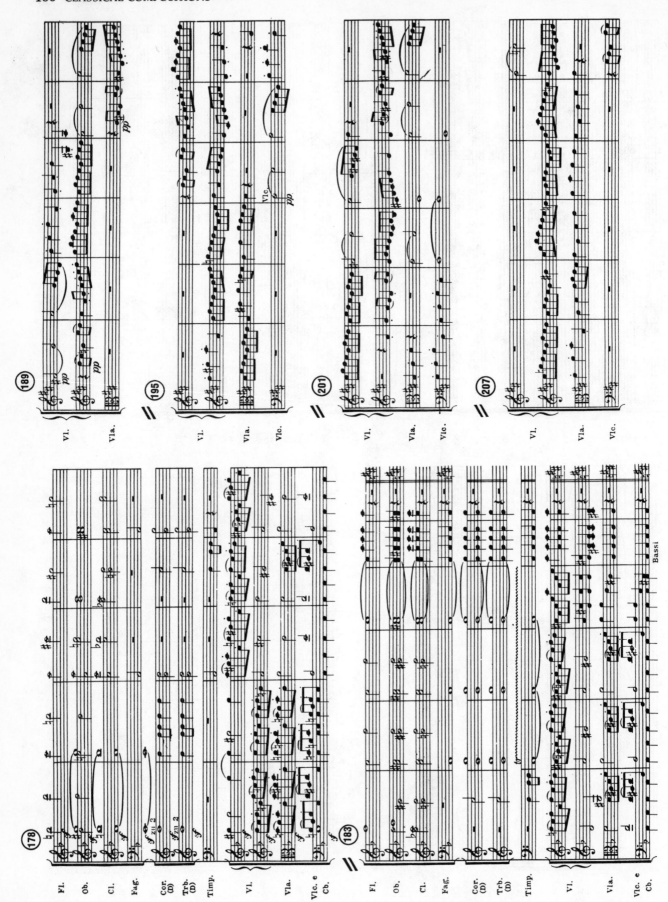

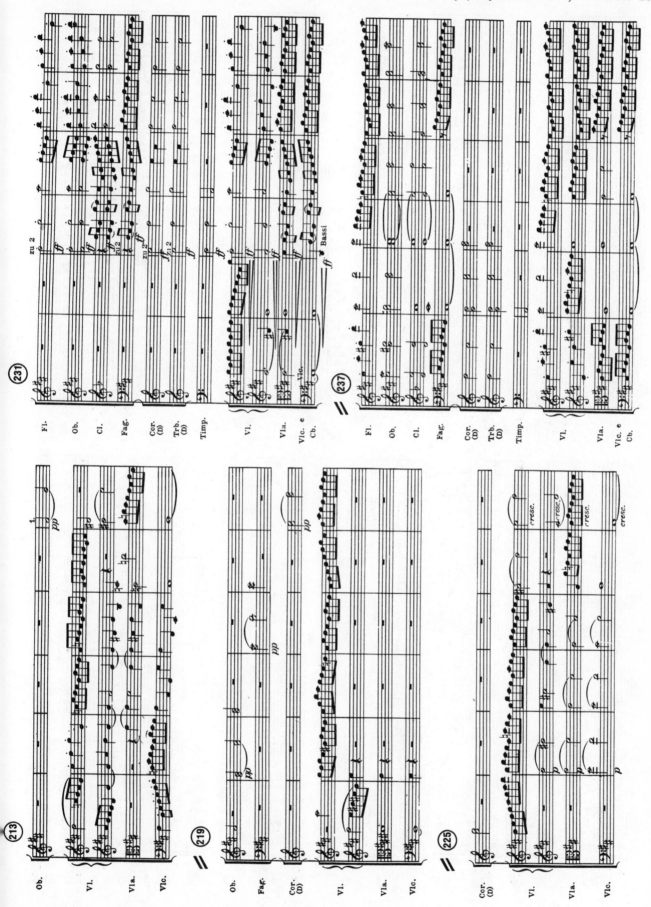

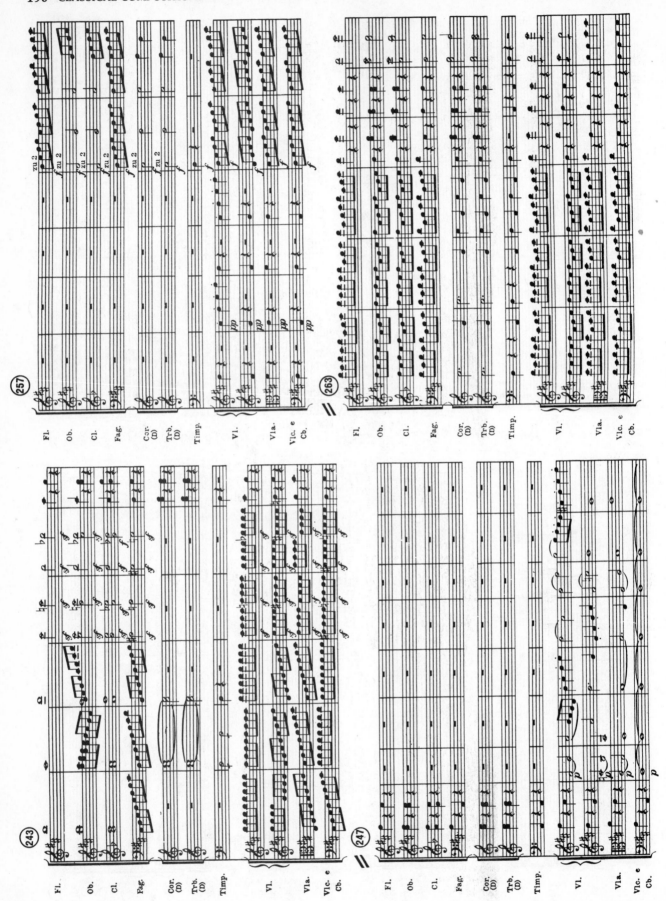

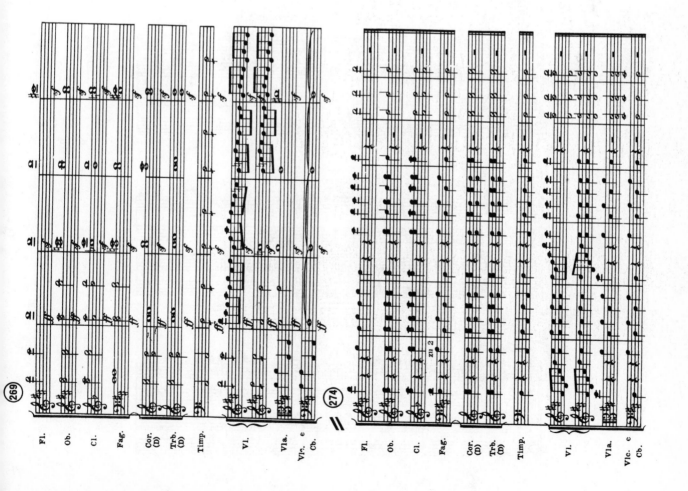

String Quartet in D minor

Op. 76, No. 2, first movement

(1799?)

Joseph Haydn

(1732–1809)

This celebrated four-movement quartet is nicknamed for the melodic fifths—*Quinten* in German—that play many roles in the first movement. Equally unusual is the thematic design of bars 118–138 and their relation to what precedes them.

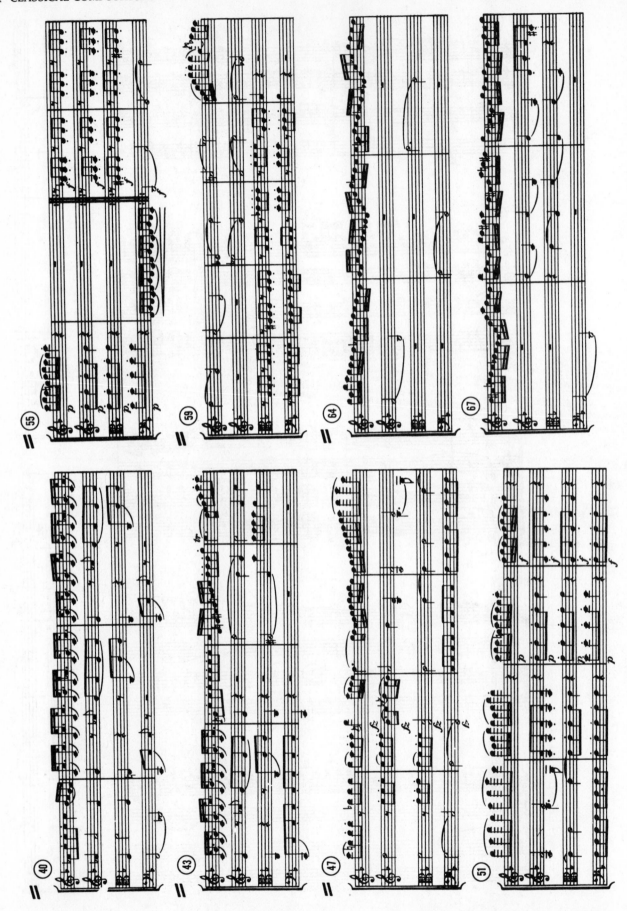

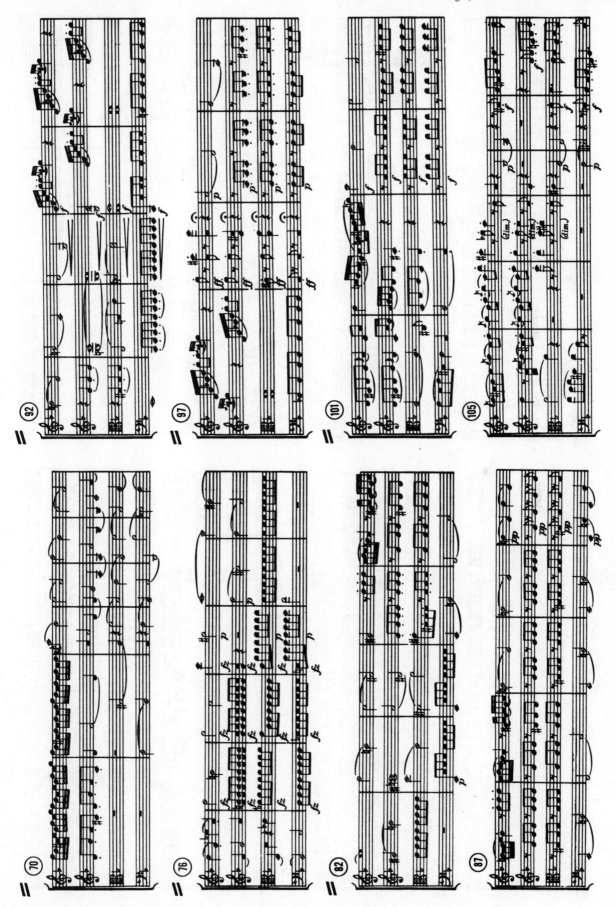

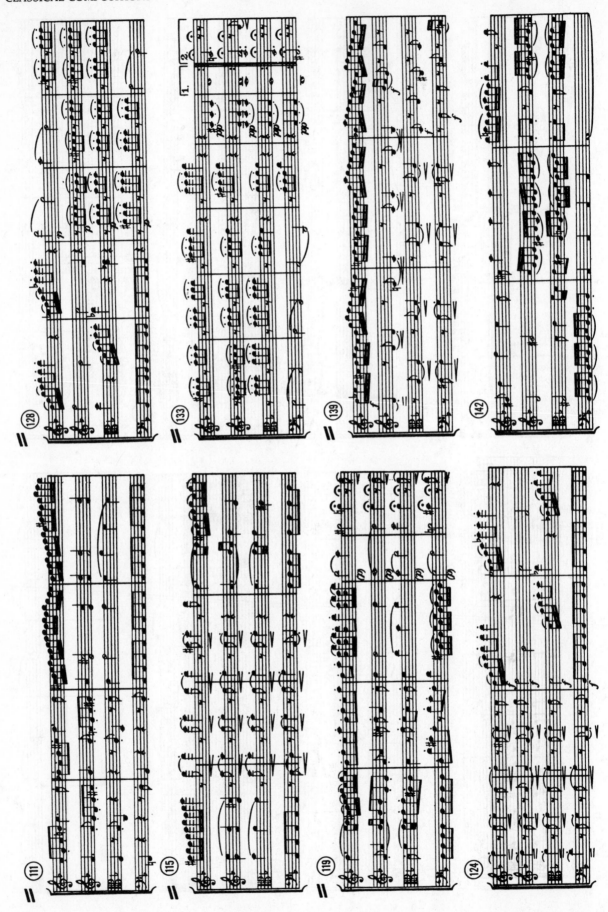

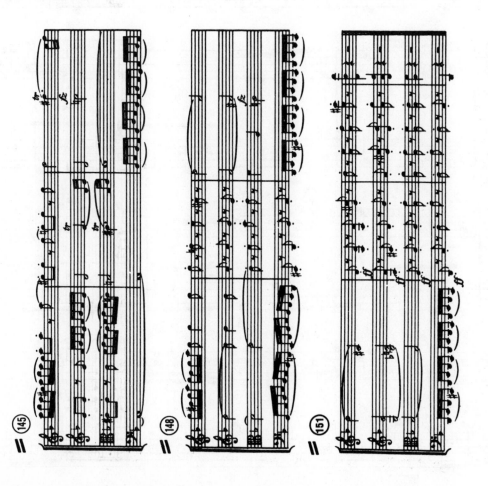

Sonatina in F major

Op. 36, No. 4, first movement

(publ. ca. 1809)

Muzio Clementi

(1752–1832)

Clementi was a musician of such achievement that he once engaged in a virtuosic keyboard joust with Mozart. Though now remembered more as a pianist than as a composer, his music is often charming and always idiomatic for its medium. This example, from a work intended for students of the piano, reveals its form with the utmost clarity. What happens when f^2, appearing first in bar 5, appears again?

Theme with Variations

from Piano Sonata in D major, K. 284

(1775)

Wolfgang Amadeus Mozart

(1756–1791)

These variations on an original theme are the third and last movement of the *Piano Sonata in D Major*, K. 284. The theme is itself an elaboration of a simple melodic and harmonic substructure—the key to the variations.

Rich in elaborative devices, the work is suffused with Mozartean wit. Note especially the amusing rhythmic effect of the "extra" measure—the thirteenth—as it appears in each variation.

For a comment on the performance of the appoggiaturas written in small notes, see the preface to the B flat major sonata, K. 333, on page 213.

Var. VIII.
Maggiore.

Var. XII.
(Allegro.)

Piano Sonata in B flat major

K. 333
(1778)

Wolfgang Amadeus Mozart
(1756–1791)

This work, given here in its entirety, has been called by Alfred Einstein a realization of the ideal of Mozart's piano sonatas.[2]

The student is reminded that the opening four notes are performed as four sixteenth notes, and that all the small appoggiaturas are played on the beat. Their length depends on their context. The one in bar 27, for example, would have the length of an eighth note; the ones in bar 7 of the second movement are thirty-seconds. Are all appoggiaturas written small? What is the advantage of so writing them?

The third movement has something of the atmosphere of a concerto: the statement of the opening eight bars *piano* and their immediate repetition *forte* suggests the way in which the finales of some of Mozart's piano concertos begin, and the cadenza near the end—rare in a solo sonata—confirms this impression. The relation of bars 76–80 to bars 16–20 might be overlooked in a cursory analysis.

²Alfred Einstein, *Mozart, His Character, His Work* (New York: Oxford University Press, 1945), p. 240.

Allegretto grazioso

Fantasia in C minor

K. 475

(1785)

Wolfgang Amadeus Mozart

(1756–1791)

In the creation of a fantasia, the composer does not adhere to a pre-established form. This is not to say that fantasias are formless, but that each is a unique form. The ideal is to control improvisatory flights by means of an over-all direction. In the bold, uninhibited fantasia given here, with its astonishing lack of key signature, how does Mozart achieve unity from such violently contrasting parts?[3]

[3]An analysis of this fantasia, with a graph showing the bass structure, is given in an article by Oswald Jonas, "Improvisation in Mozarts Klavierwerken," in *Mozart Jahrbuch* (Salzburg: Internationalen Stiftung Mozarteum, 1967), pp. 179–181. Another is given by Felix Salzer in his *Structural Hearing* (New York: Dover Publications, 1962), Vol. 2, Graph 507.

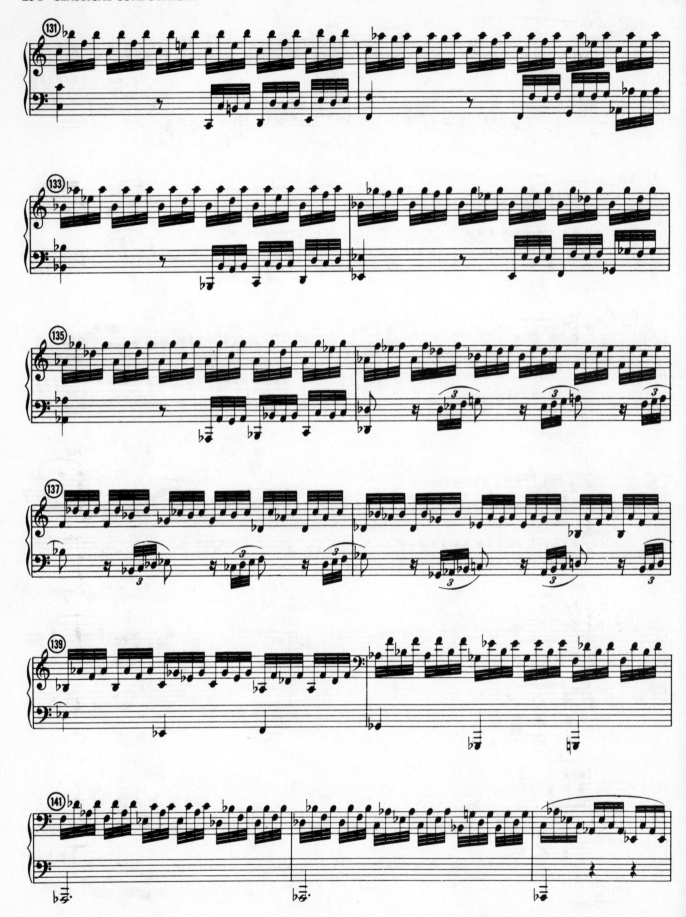

144
(decresc.)
(p)
(p)
147
151
155
(ral
(sf p)
(sf p)
159
len
tan
do)
(sf p)
163
Tempo primo.
f
p
(pp)

Piano Concerto in C minor
K. 491, first movement
(1786)

Wolfgang Amadeus Mozart
(1756–1791)

This eloquent, tragic movement is the largest single form given in this anthology. As a means of clearly conceptualizing the form as a whole, it is recommended that one make a diagram of the entire piece showing the location and key of each thematic material and the medium (soloist or orchestra) to which each material is assigned. In considering these broad dimensions, remember that a minute or two of music is missing at bar 486, third beat. Mozart composed nothing for this spot. Also, the soloist's part may be only sketched at bars 261 and 262, and 467 through 470.

As always in Mozart, there are also many individual details that will richly repay close inspection. See, for example, the unusual chromaticism of the opening theme (likewise bars 220 through 241), and the imaginative treatment of a familiar sequence at bars 74 through 81.

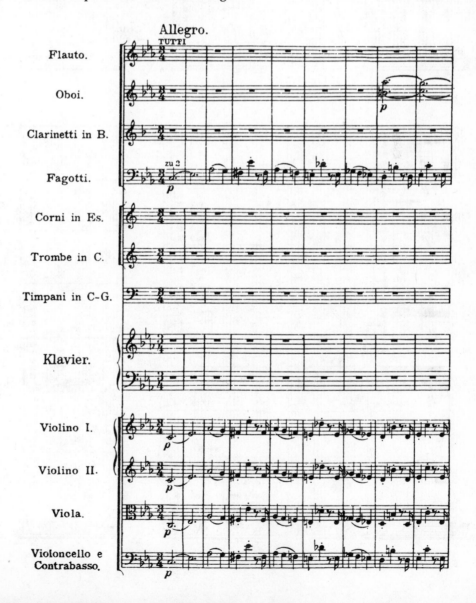

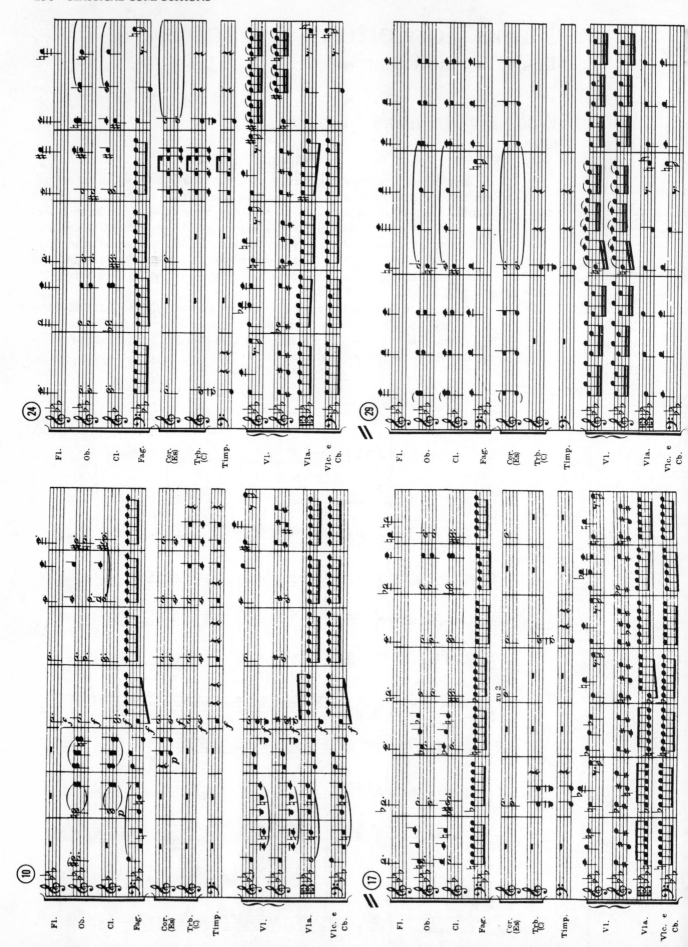

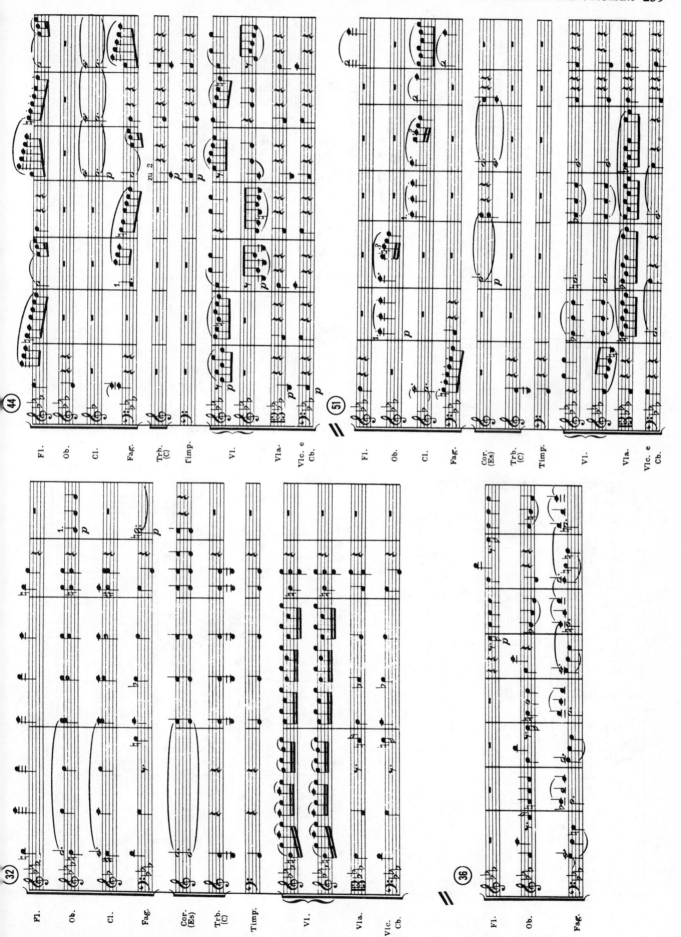

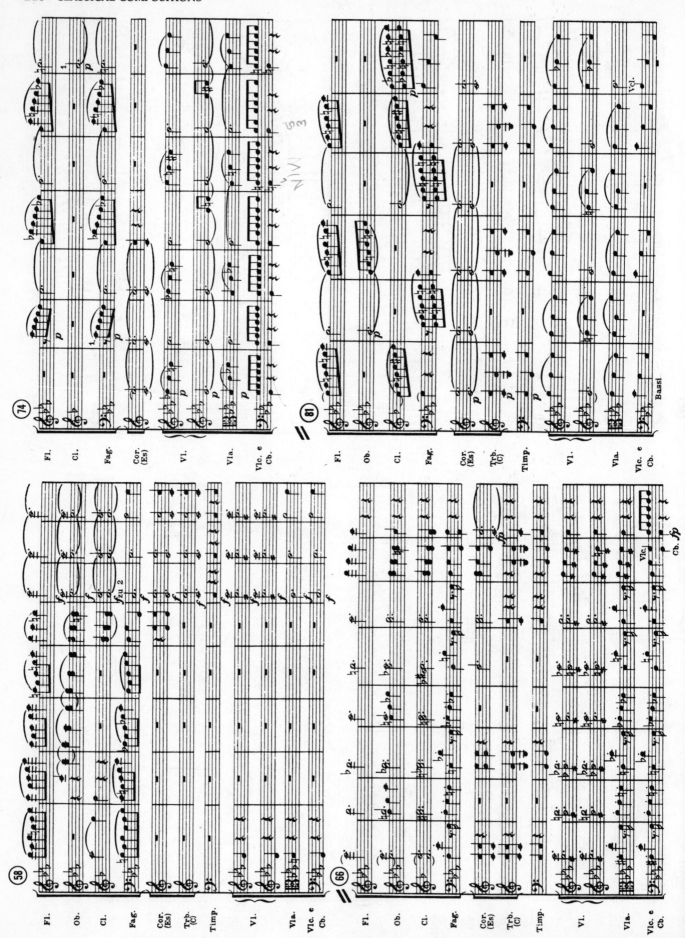

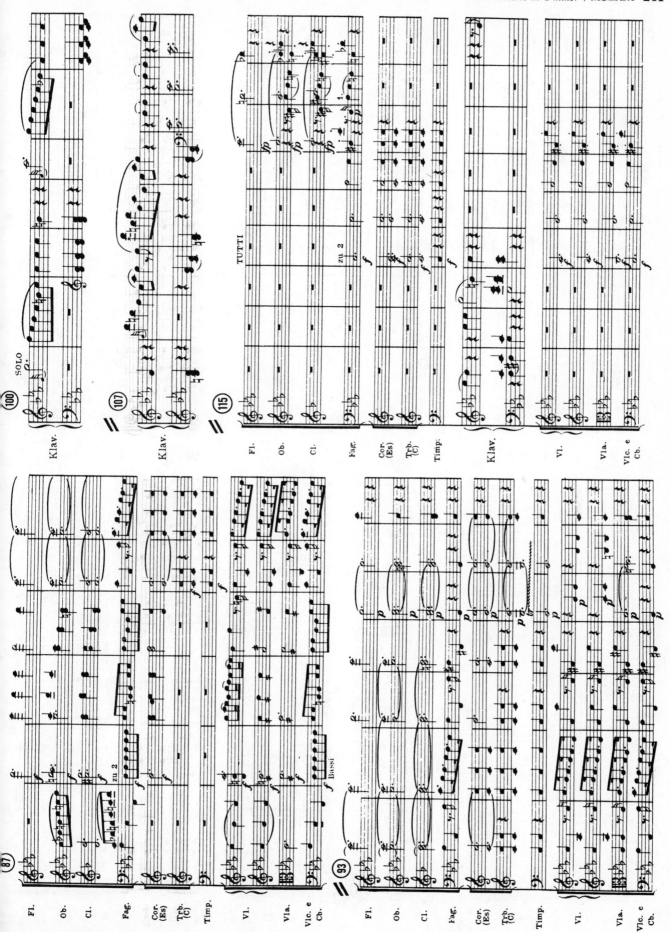

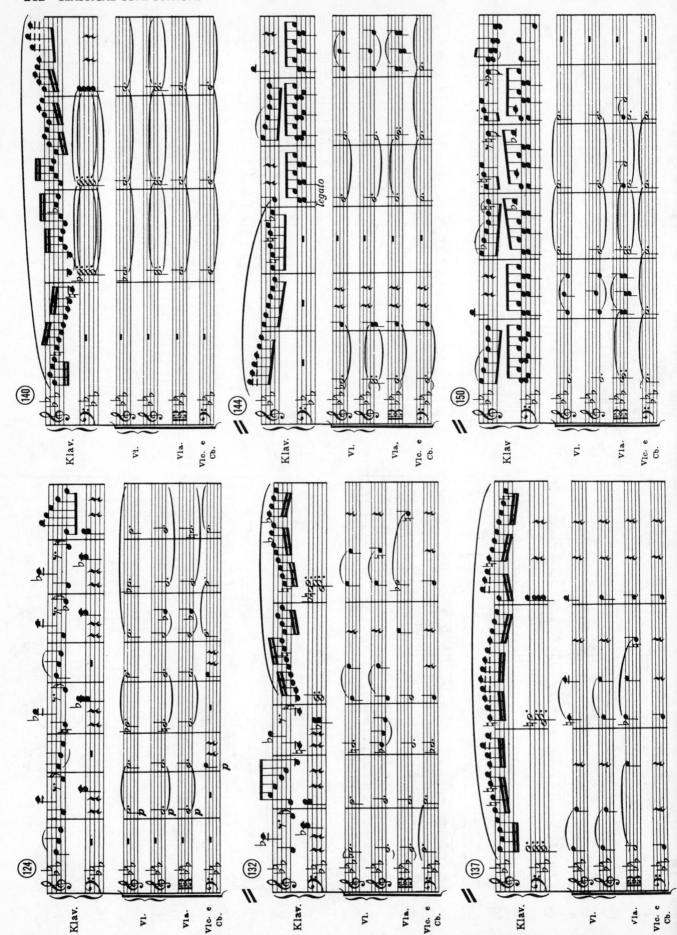

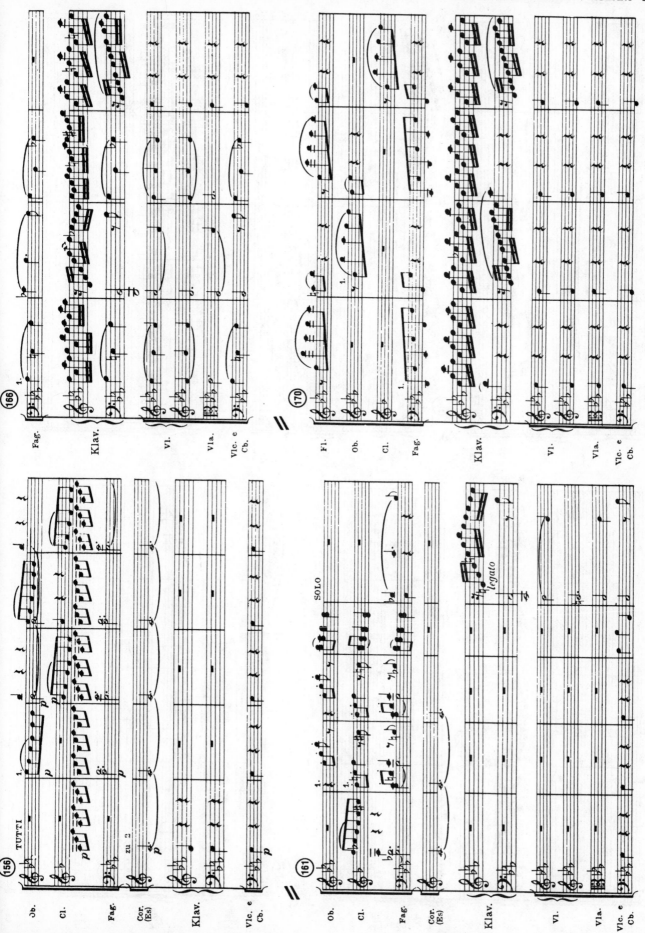

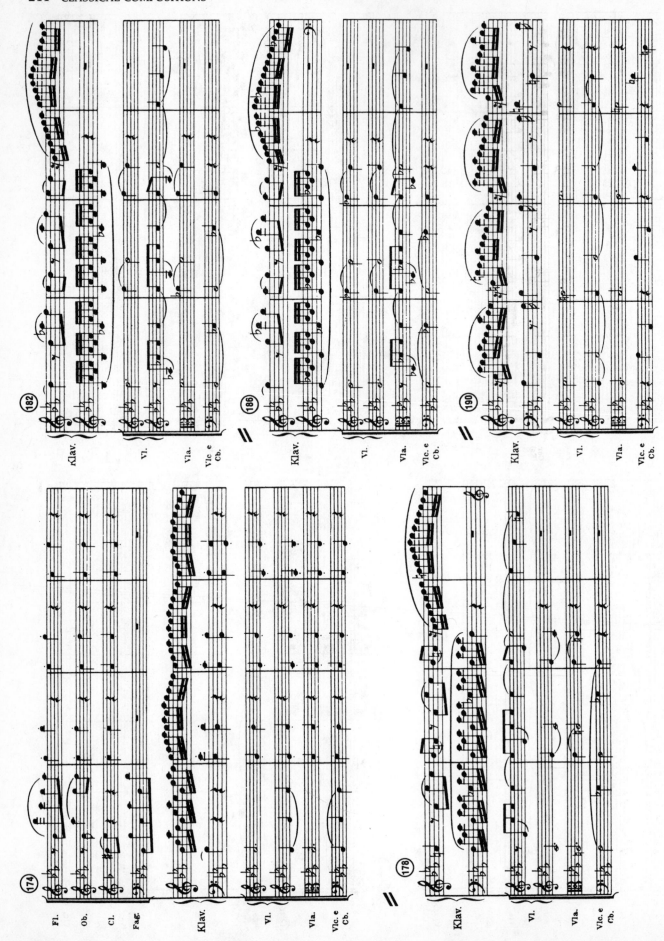

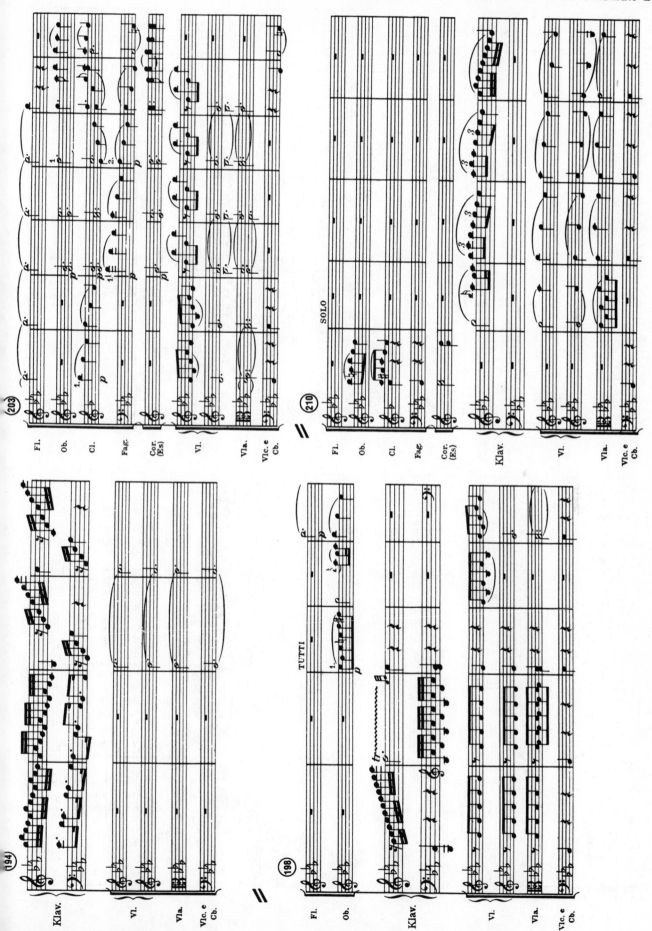

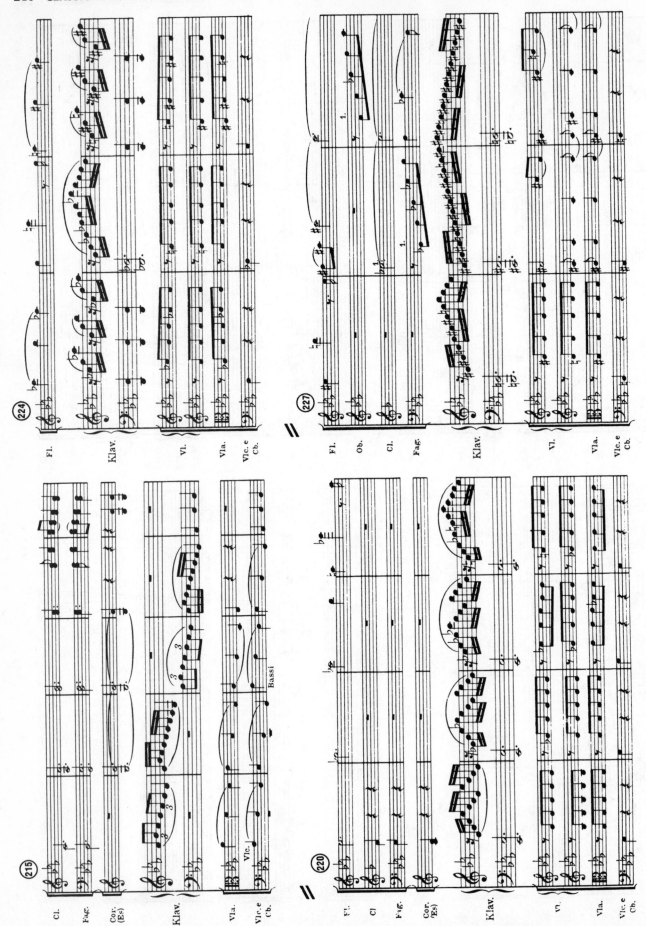

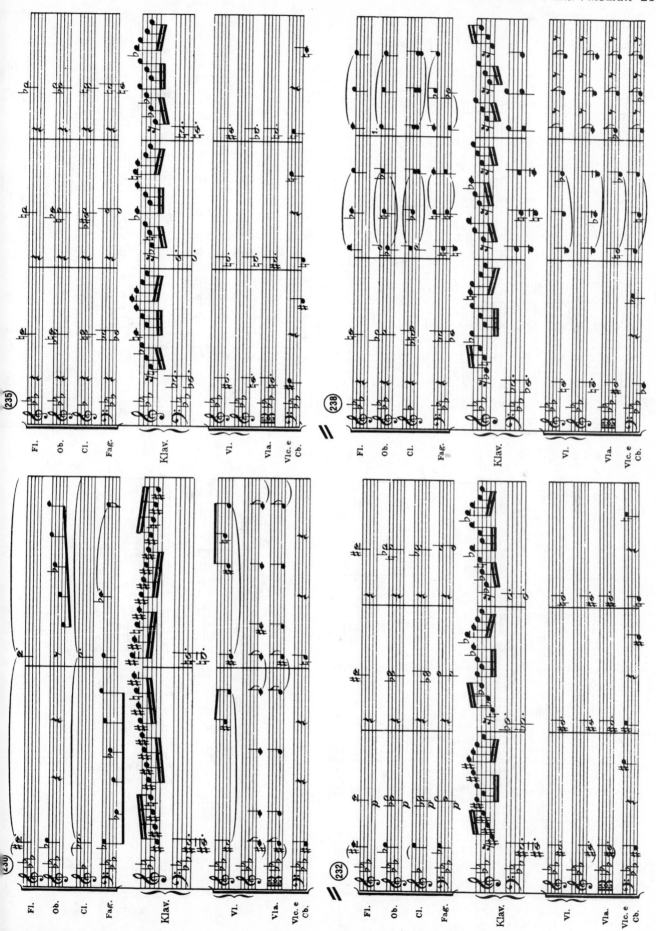

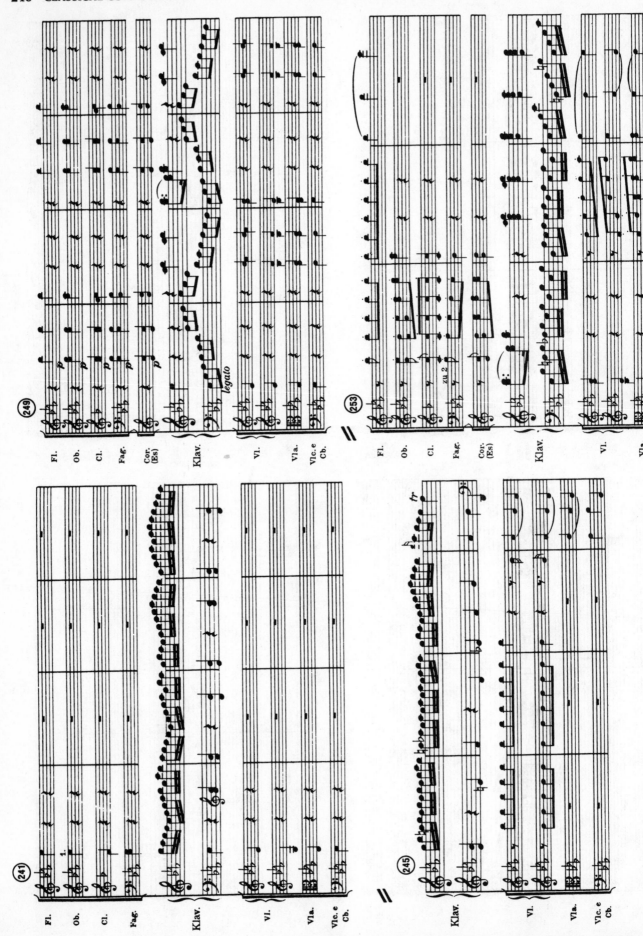

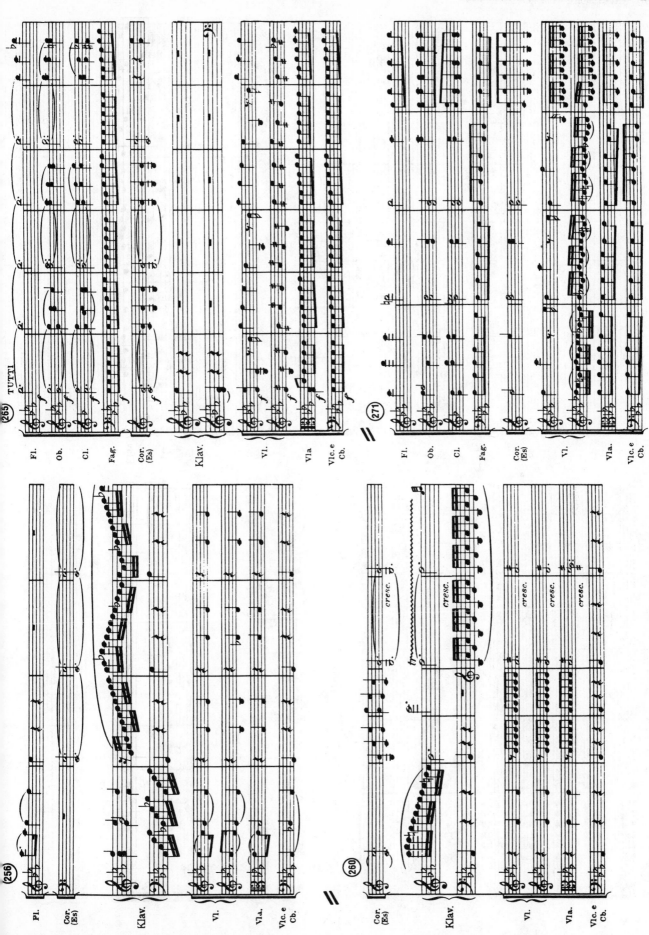

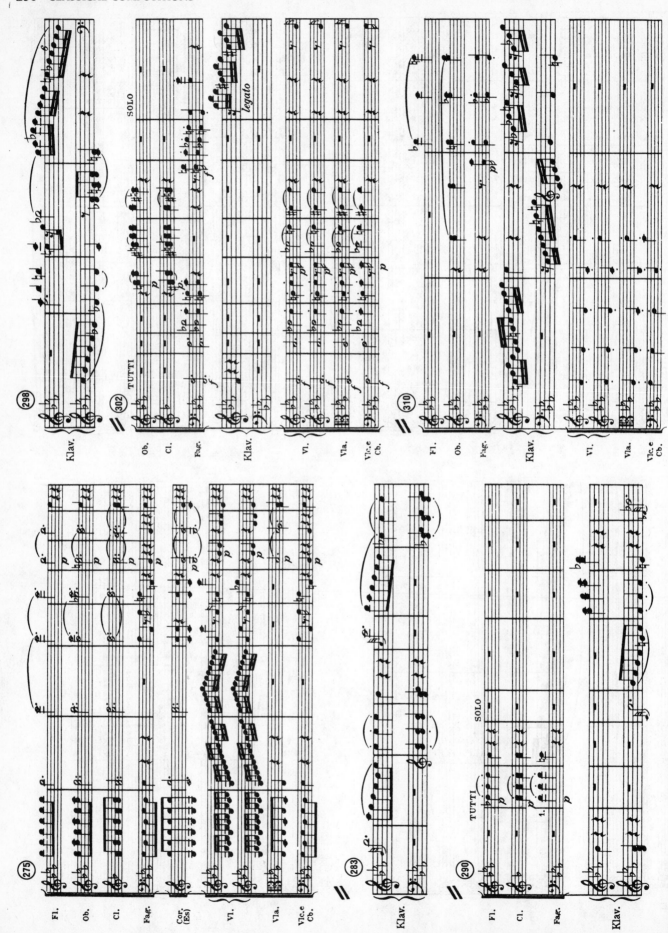

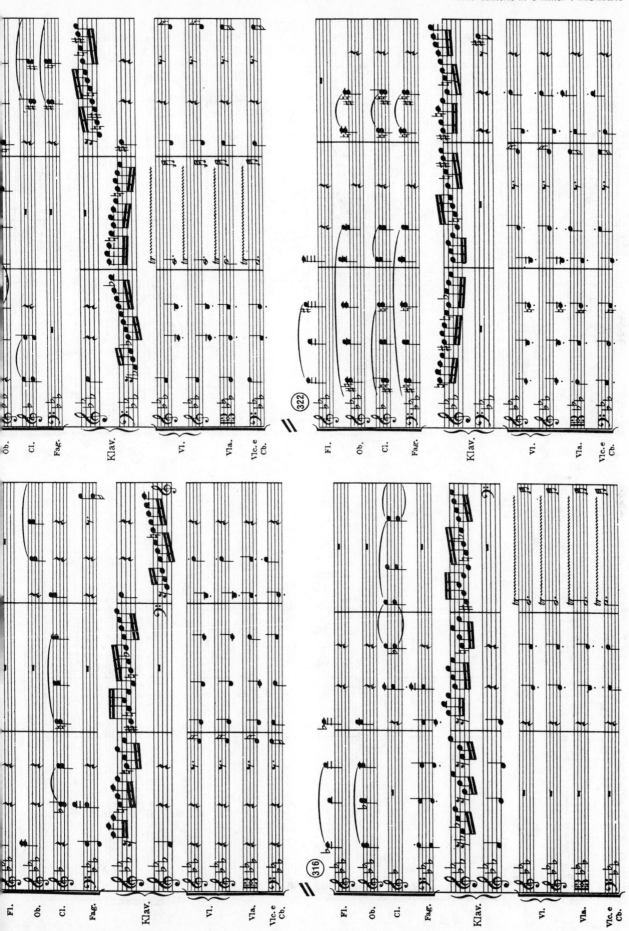

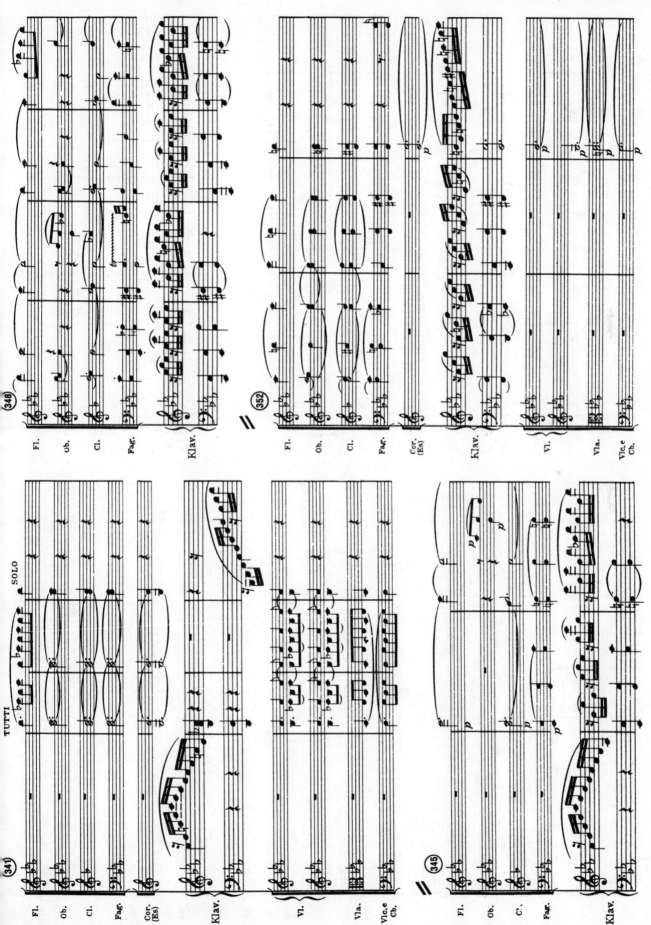

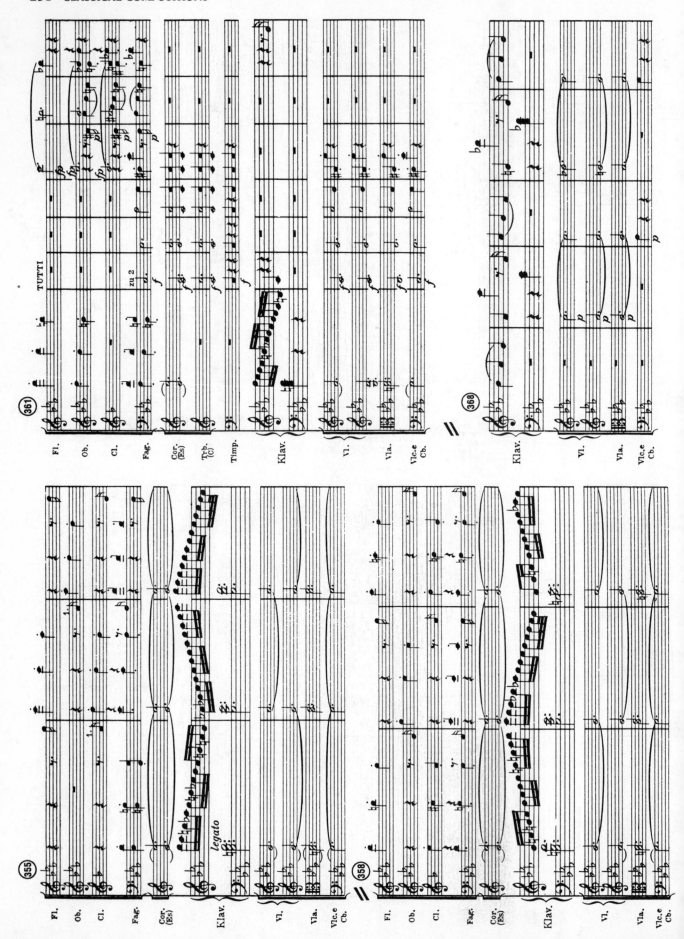

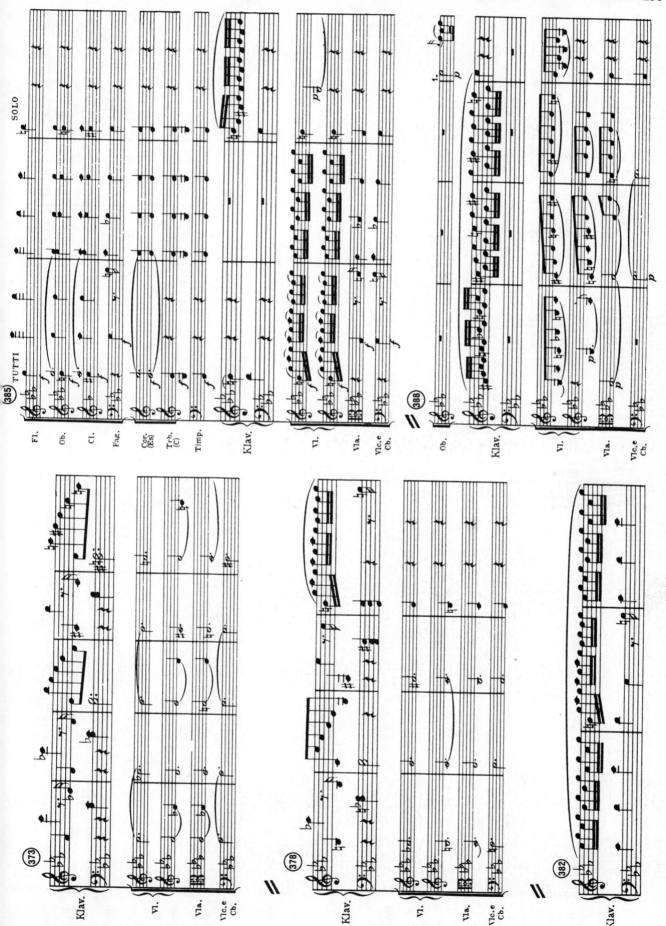

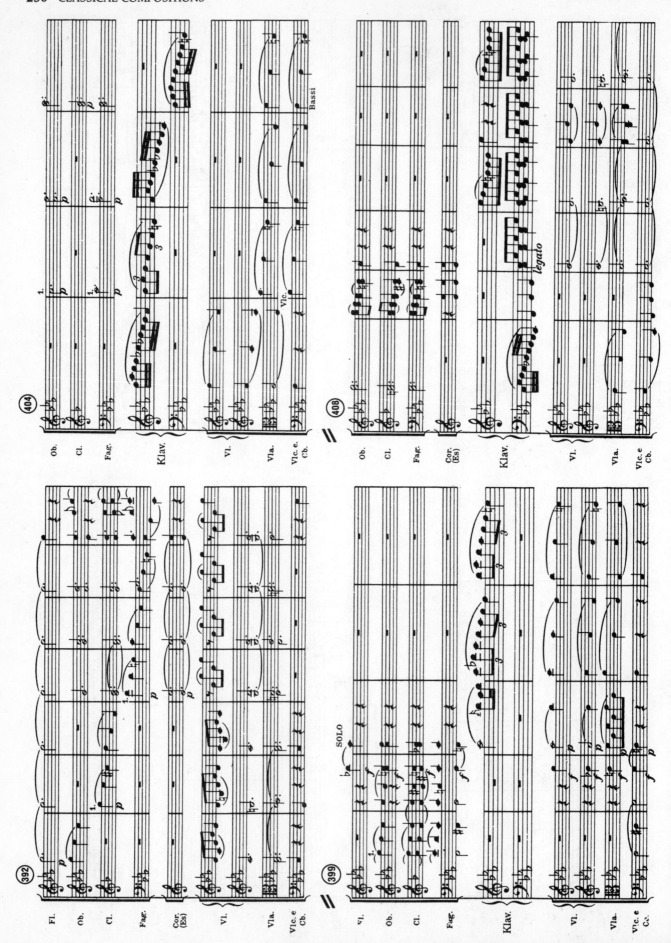

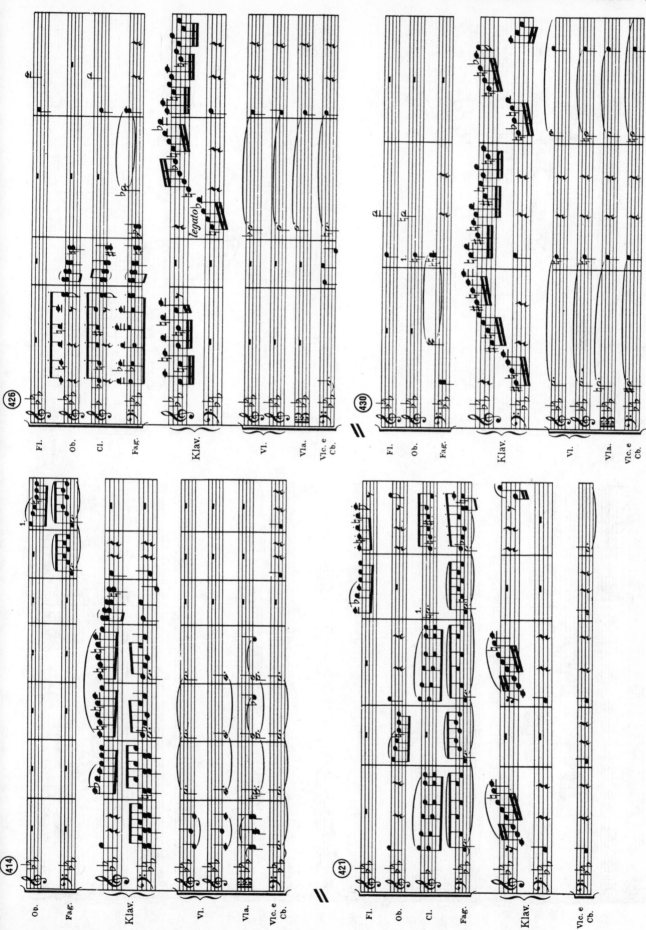

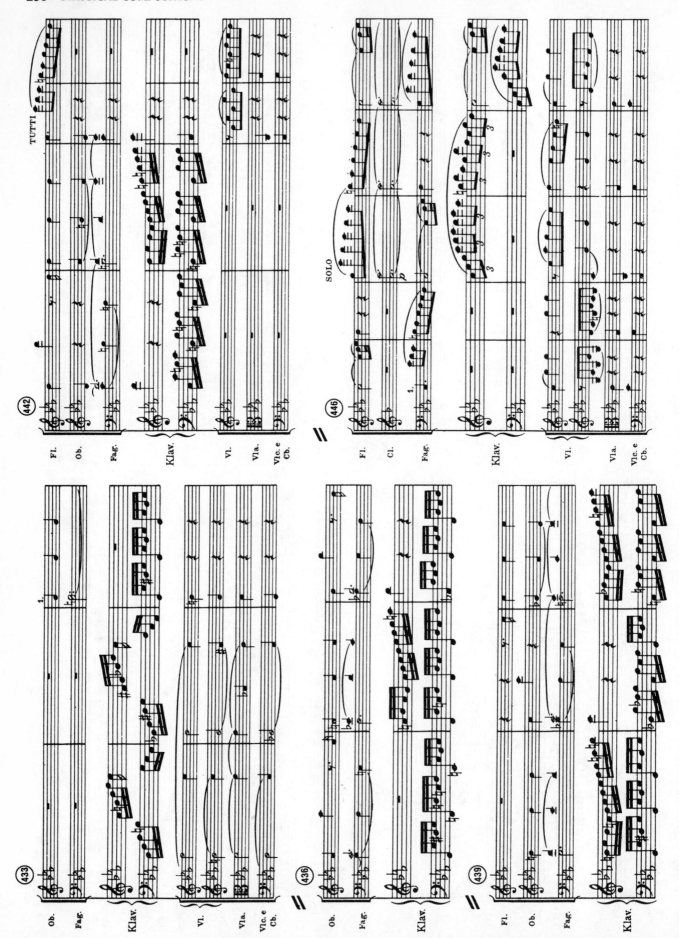

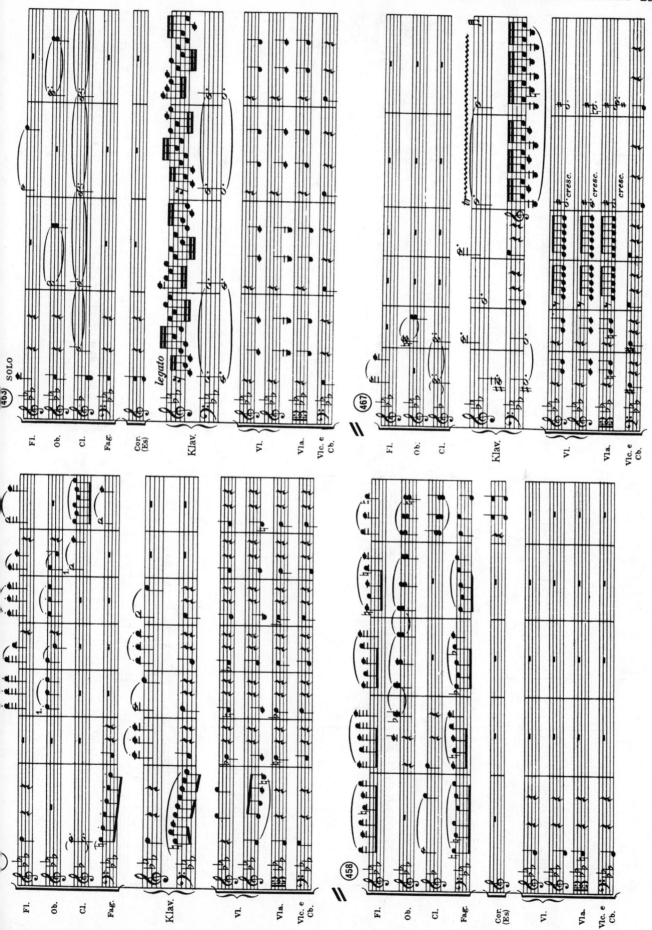

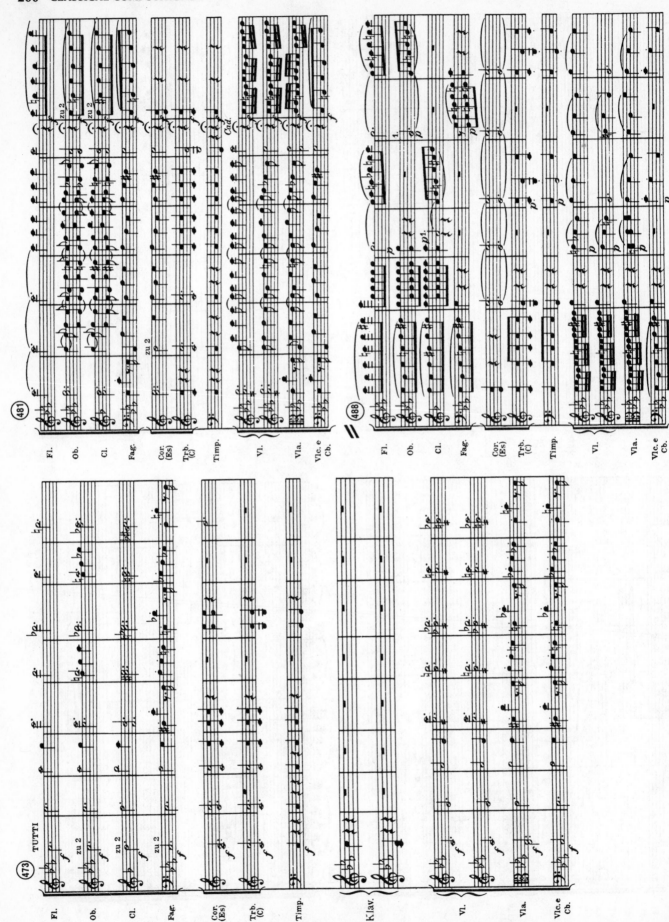

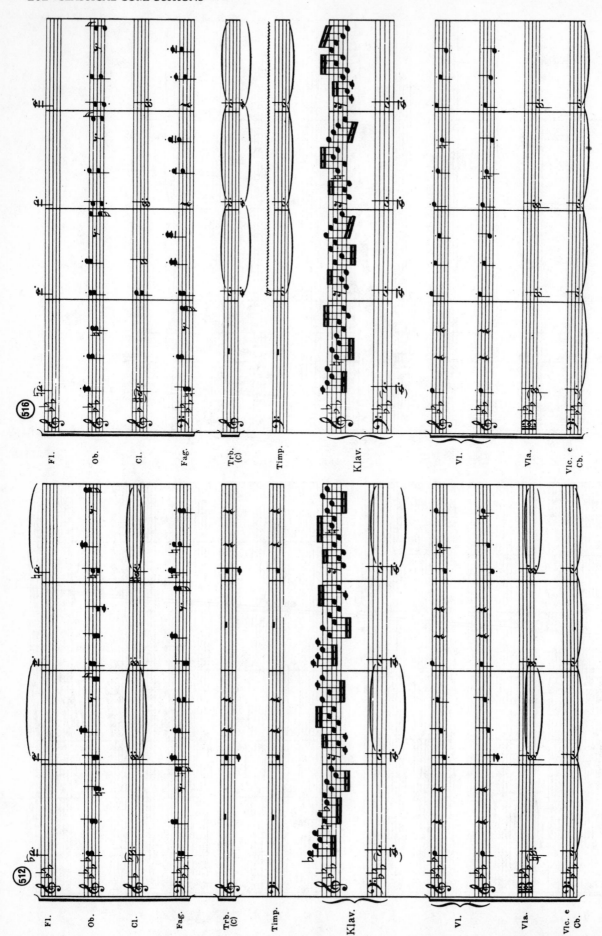

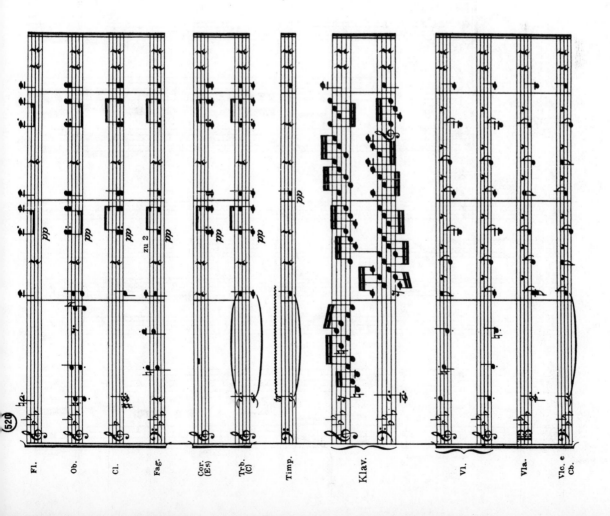

Kyrie eleison

from *Requiem*, K. 626

(1791)

Wolfgang Amadeus Mozart

(1756–1791)

Mozart's immortal requiem mass was unfortunately left incomplete at his death. The opening number begins *Adagio* with the words of the *Requiem aeternam,* then concludes with the excerpt given here. Not only is this a double fugue, but the two subjects of the fugue display a special type of invertible counterpoint. To discover this, examine carefully the relation of the two subjects to each other throughout the piece. Also consider this music from a stylistic point of view. Would you guess it was by Mozart? Other post-Baroque fugues are given on pages 188 (at bar 189), 517, and 544.

Piano Sonata No. 1 in F minor

Op. 2, No. 1, first and third movements
(1795?)

Ludwig van Beethoven
(1770–1827)

Elementary musical analysis will rightly be concerned with thematic design, formal sections, and broad tonal structure. A later stage of study might take account of motivic relationships such as that between bar 2 and bars 140 through 142 of this movement: In the latter bars the right-hand part describes the turn (rhythmically augmented) that first occurs in bar 2 and is characteristic of the first theme and bridge. Similar rhythmic transformations—in F minor and one other key—of the motive C—B♭—A♭—G—F—E♮, which first appears in bars 7 and 8, will also be found throughout this movement.[4]

First Movement

[4]A bar-by-bar reduction of the entire sonata, showing both the basic rhythm of each bar and the basic voice-leading, is given by Heinrich Schenker in the second issue of *Der Tonwille* (Vienna: A. Gutmann Verlag, 1922; republished by Universal Edition).

Each movement of all 32 sonatas receive detailed description in Donald Francis Tovey's *A Companion to Beethoven's Pianoforte Sonatas* (London: The Associated Board of the R.A.M. and the R.C.M., 1931).

Third Movement

What is the harmony and essential voice leading of the first two bars? Of bars 25 through 28? Compare the form of bars 1 through 40 with that of the trio, and the entire movement with other pieces with "trio." (See "Trio" in the General Index.) Pianists will want to assess the fingering in bars 59 through 62 because it is Beethoven's own. Does it have musical, as opposed to merely physical, advantages?[5]

[5]Jeanne Bamberger treats this interesting question in her article, "The Musical Significance of Beethoven's Fingerings in the Piano Sonatas," *The Music Forum*, Vol. IV (New York: Columbia University Press, 1976), p. 237.

Trio

Men.D.C.

Piano Sonata No. 3 in C major

Op. 2, No. 3, third movement

(1795?)

Ludwig van Beethoven

(1770–1827)

The scherzo came to replace the minuet in many of Beethoven's sonatas and other several-movement works. Like the minuet, it was originally the third of four movements, but later this order was often changed. This example should be compared with the minuets in this book as well as with the scherzos on pages 295 and 324. Its rich display of mode mixture also invites analysis. Explain the D flats in the final phrase.

Scherzo D. C.
e poi la Coda.

Coda

Piano Sonata No. 4 in E flat major

Op. 7, second movement

(1796–1797?)

Ludwig van Beethoven

(1770–1827)

Study the form of this music of *"gran espressione."* How does it differ from that of the Beethoven slow movement on page 283, which was composed at about the same time?

[6]Insightful comment on this movement is given by Roger Kamien in his article "Chromatic Details in Beethoven's Op. 7," in *The Music Review* (August, 1974), p. 149.

Piano Sonata No. 5 in C minor

Op. 10, No. 1, second movement
(1796–1798)

Ludwig van Beethoven
(1770–1827)

Sonata No. 5 was the first of Beethoven's sonatas to have three, rather than four, movements. This movement reveals a form that he used more than once for slow movements. What is the relation of bars 24–27 to 28–31? After bar 31, where is the first full cadence? What is the significance of the chord in bar 45?

Piano Sonata No. 8 in C minor

Op. 13, third movement

(1798–1799)

Ludwig van Beethoven

(1770–1827)

This movement closes the well-known *Pathétique* sonata. What is its form? What occasional resemblances does its form have to sonata form? What is the relation of bars 79—80 to 83—84? Of 99—100 to 103—104? What small form is represented by bars 79—107?

Piano Sonata No. 15 in D major

Op. 28, third movement

(1801)

Ludwig van Beethoven

(1770–1827)

Consider the extreme terseness of the musical language here. Also compare the form of the scherzo section with that of the trio. How does the form of the trio differ from that of the trios of other minuets and scherzos in this book? Why does Beethoven say to play the last 16 bars only one time—*"una volta"*?

La seconda parte una volta

Scherzo da capo.

Piano Sonata No. 17 in D minor
Op. 31, No. 2, first movement
(1802)

Ludwig van Beethoven
(1770–1827)

This sonata has been nicknamed "The Tempest" because of a casual reference by Beethoven to Shakespeare's play of the same name. Discover the very unusual features of this stormy, romantic music. What is the form? Is it meaningful to view the piece in terms of some traditional form?[7]

[7]Roger Kamien analyzes extensive portions of this movement in his article "Aspects of the Recapitulation in Beethoven Piano Sonatas," *The Music Forum*, Vol. IV (New York: Columbia University Press, 1976), p. 228ff.

Piano Sonata No. 21 in C major

Op. 53, first movement

(1803–1804)

Ludwig van Beethoven

(1770–1827)

Dedicated to a patron, Count von Waldstein, and often identified by his name, this sonata opens with a tumultuous allegro of great scope. What is unusual about its form?[8]

[8]Portions of this movement are analyzed in Kamien, "Aspects," *op. cit.,* p. 205ff.

String Quartet No. 16 in F major
Op. 135
(1826)

Ludwig van Beethoven
(1770–1827)

Beethoven's last string quartet—and almost his last composition—is given below in its entirety. Though traditional forms are evident throughout the work, each movement also has many unusual features of structure and design.

On his manuscript, at the beginning of the last movement, Beethoven wrote the inscription, "The Decision Made with Difficulty," and followed this with, "Must it be? It must be!" How does the music interpret these words? That is, how does it feel about them?

Lento assai, cantante e tranquillo.

Più lento.

DER SCHWER GEFASSTE ENTSCHLUSS.

Muss es sein? / Es muss sein! / Es muss sein!
Must it be? / *It must be!* / *It must be!*

PART FOUR

Compositions of the Romantic Era

The Song Forms.   A large and varied selection of two- and three-part "song forms" will be found in this section. Such forms occur in Part Three as well, but there they are usually imbedded in larger forms. Here they are complete compositions. To locate examples, begin with the entry "Song Forms" in the General Index.

Chromaticism.   This section also provides many examples of ninetenth-century chromaticism. Pieces that are quite chromatic all or most of the way through are Chopin's *Preludes 2, 4,* and *9,* and his *Mazurka 49,* the *Prelude* and *Liebestod* from Wagner's *Tristan,* the violin sonata movement of Franck, and Wolf's *In dem Schatten meiner Locken* and *In der Frühe.* In addition, many other pieces contain strikingly chromatic passages. An effort has been made to make all this material as useful as possible to students and teachers of chromatic harmony by citing many individual details either in the General Index under entries beginning with the word "Chromatically," or in the chromatic section of the Index of Chords, Sequences, and Modulations. The chromatic pieces in Part Four may be compared with highly chromatic tonal works in other parts of the book, notably Debussy's *Prelude to "Afternoon of a Faun,"* Mozart's C minor fantasia, Bach's *Crucifixus,* the Handel recitative from *Messiah,* as well as the Gesualdo madrigal and the excerpt from the *Prophetiae Sibyllarum* of Lassus.

The Lieder.   Musicians, who so frequently think of a song only in terms of its music, sometimes need to remind themselves that in most cases the words existed first, and that a composer, before writing a note, must be deeply aware of the text's meaning, or at least some aspect of it. Singers know how necessary it is to understand the words before a valid interpretation of a song is possible. Likewise anyone who studies a song seriously will attempt to discover how the text is expressed in the music. One consideration is the relation of a poem's form to the musical form. Another is the way in which a song may express some aspect of the meaning of the poem. I refer not only to mere "text painting" or to general mood, but to a relation between the poem's content and the music's structure. Not all songs have this attribute, and those that do have it manifest it in very different ways. A vivid example is Schubert's *Erlkonig.*

There are ten *lieder* in Part Four, selected to show—among many other, more interesting, things—various types of strophic, modified strophic, and through-composed treatment. For the sake of accuracy in meaning, texts not originally in English are provided with literal rather than singable translations.

Three Songs

Franz Schubert

(1797–1828)

Who is Sylvia?—Op. 106, No. 4 (D. 891)

(1826)

Text: William Shakespeare's Two Gentlemen of Verona

The words of this tender song are given here in the language of the poet who wrote them, since the German translation used by Schubert had the same line and rhyme scheme. Each stanza has only five lines; Schubert repeated the fifth. What is the musical form? What is unusual about the constructuion of the individual phrases?

Moderato

pp

⑤

pp

1. Who   is   Syl - via?   What   is   she, ___   That
2. Is   she   kind ___   as   she   is   fair? ___   For
3. Then   to   Syl - via   let   us   sing, ___   That

⑨

all   our swains com - mend   her?   Ho -   ly,
beau - ty   lives with   kind - ness: Love   doth
Syl - via   is   ex - cel - ling;   She   ex -

fair,____ and__ wise is she;____ The heav'n such grace did
to____ her__ eyes re - pair,____ To help him of his
cels____ each__ mor - tal thing____ Up - on the dull earth

lend _____ her, That she__ might____ ad -
blind - ness; And be - ing help'd____ in -
dwell - ing: To her __ let us

mir - ed _____ be, That she
hab - its _____ there, Be - ing
gar - lands _____ bring, To her

might   ad   -   mir   -   ed___   be.
help'd   in   -   hab   -   its___   there.
let   us   gar   -   lands___ bring.

Der Doppelgänger (from *Schwanengesang*, D. 957)

(1828)

Text: Heinrich Heine

How are the three poetic stanzas treated in "The Double," one of Schubert's last, and most powerful, songs?

Still is the night, the streets are calm,
In this house lived my treasure;
She long ago left this town,
But the house still stands in the same place.

There stands also a man, and stares into the heavens,
And wrings his hands for pain;
I shudder when his face I see,
[For] the moon shows me my own features.
Thou double, thou pale companion!
Why do you ape the love-sorrows
That tortured me in this place
So many nights in times gone by?

Nacht, in al - - - ter Zeit?

Erlkönig—Op. 1 (D. 328)

(1815)

Text: Johann Wolfgang von Goethe

The close relation of the over-all tonal scheme to the meaning of the text contributes much to the extraordinary effect of this song, composed when Schubert was eighteen.

Who rides so late through night and wind?
It is a father with his child;
He holds the boy in his arm,
He clasps him tight, he keeps him warm.

"My son, why hidest thy face in fear?"
"Seest thou not, Father, the Erlking?
The Erlking with crown and train?"
"My son, 'tis but a streak of mist."

"O dear child, come away with me!
Lovely games I'll play with thee!
Many-colored flowers grow by the shore,
My mother has many golden robes."

"My father, my father, hearest thou not
What Erlking softly promises me?"
"Be calm, be calm, my child;
In the withered leaves rustles the wind."

"Fair boy, wilt thou come with me?
My lovely daughters shall wait on thee;
My daughters keep their nightly revels;
They will rock thee, dance, and sing thee to sleep."

"My father, my father, seest thou not
Erlking's daughters in that dark place?"
"My son, my son, I see clearly;
It is only the gleam of the old gray willows."

"I love thee, thy fair form ravishes me;
And if thou art not willing, I'll take thee by force."
"My father, my father, now he is seizing me!
Erlking has done me harm!"

The father shudders, he rides fast,
And holds in his arm the moaning child;
He reaches home with effort and toil:
In his arms the child lay dead!

Moment Musical No. 6 in A flat major

from *Sechs Moments Musicaux*, Op. 94 (D. 780)

(ca. 1825)

Franz Schubert

(1797–1828)

Account for the many C flats and F flats throughout the *Allegretto,* as well as the C naturals in bars 35 and 38, and the two changes to four-sharp signature. What is the function of the diminished-seventh chords in bars 34 and 101? How does the section starting at bar 40 contribute to the form of bars 1 through 77? What is the form of the entire composition?

Allegretto D.C.

Song Without Words

Op. 62, No. 1

(1844)

Felix Mendelssohn

(1809–1847)

"Song Without Words" *(Lied ohne Worte)* is the title Mendelssohn gave to each of 48 short piano pieces of markedly song-like character that he wrote at various periods of his life. In the example given here, discover the various sections and how they are melodically and harmonically related. What is the form? How is the piece an unusual example of that form?

Seven Pieces

from *Album for the Young,* Op. 68
(1848)

Robert Schumann
(1810–1856)

Like many composers before and since, Schumann wrote music for his own children to play. The following selection of pieces from his *Album for the Young* starts out easy and becomes increasingly challenging—both to play and to analyze.

1—Melodie (Melody)

3—Trällerliedchen (Humming Song)

6—Armes Waisenkind (Poor Orphan Child)

8—Wilder Reiter (The Wild Rider)

14—Kleine Studie (Short Study)

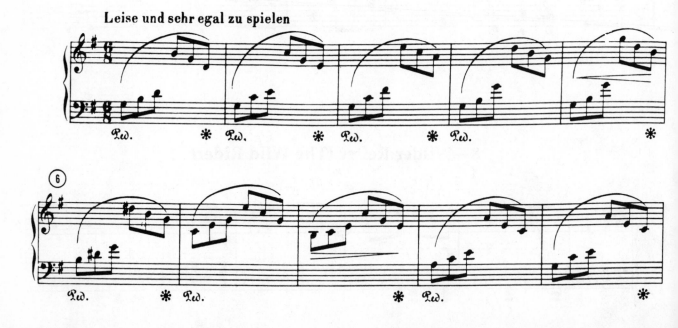

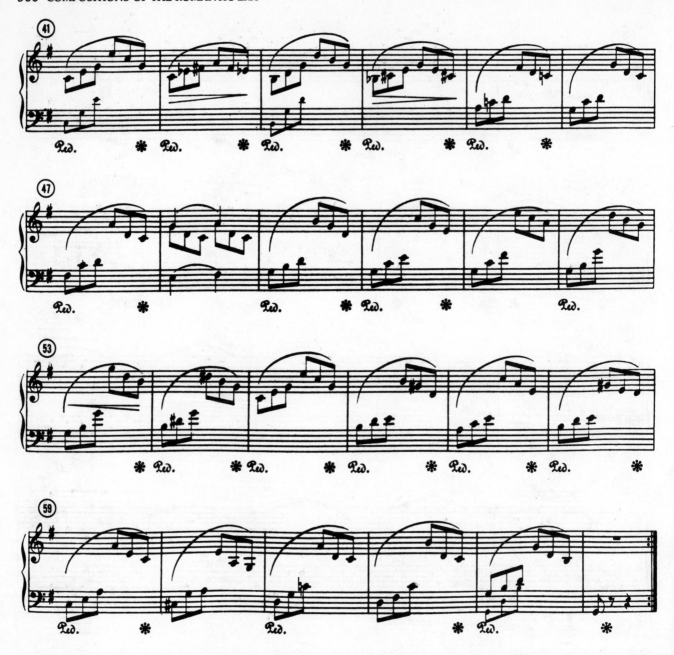

17—Kleiner Morgenwanderer (Little Morning Wanderer)

31—Kriegslied (War Song)

Vogel als Prophet

from *Waldszenen*, Op. 82

(1848–1849)

Robert Schumann

(1810–1856)

The Prophetic Bird from the character-piece cycle *Forest Scenes* is a typically Schumannesque study in biting dissonance. Explain the dissonances, especially the crunches in bars 11 and 13—14. Is the first note of the piece dissonant? What is the form of bars 1 through 18? Of the entire piece? Consider the use of the soft pedal (*Verschiebung*) in bars 23—24, and the fact that it is not called for anywhere else.

Ich grolle nicht

from *Dichterliebe*, Op. 48

(1840)

Robert Schumann

(1810–1856)

Text: Heinrich Heine

Another example of highly expressive dissonance, but one quite different from *Vogel als Prophet* (see page 364), is afforded by this song. Especially noteworthy are bars 5 through 12 and their relation to the rest of the song.[8]

Our translation follows Heine's poem exactly. Examine Schumann's adaptation of the words.

I'll not complain (bear a grudge), though my heart break,
O love ever lost! I'll not complain.
Though thou dost gleam in jewelled splendor,
There falls no ray upon thy heart's night.

I've known it long. (For) I saw thee in dream,
And saw the night within thy heart's domain,
And saw the serpent that devours thy heart:
I saw, my love, how miserable thou art.

Reprinted from Peters Edition No. 2383a. Reprint permission granted by the publisher, C. F. Peters Corporation, 373 Park Avenue South, New York, N. Y. 10016.

[8]Bars 5–12 are analyzed by William Mitchell in his *Elementary Harmony* 2d ed. (Englewood Cliffs: Prentice-Hall, Inc., 1948), pp. 179–181. *See also* Arthur Komar's edition of Schumann's *Dichterliebe* in the Norton Critical Scores series (New York: W. W. Norton & Company, 1971), pp. 82–83 and 117–118.

Preludes (Excerpts)

Op. 28
(1836–1839)

Frédéric Chopin
(1810–1849)

In terms of both piano writing and musical structure, these aphoristic statements are among the most original creations in the Romantic literature.

Prelude 1 in C major

In the right-hand part of this prelude, what effects are produced by the changes from two triplets to one quintuplet per bar? Where is the final cadence and what is happening there?

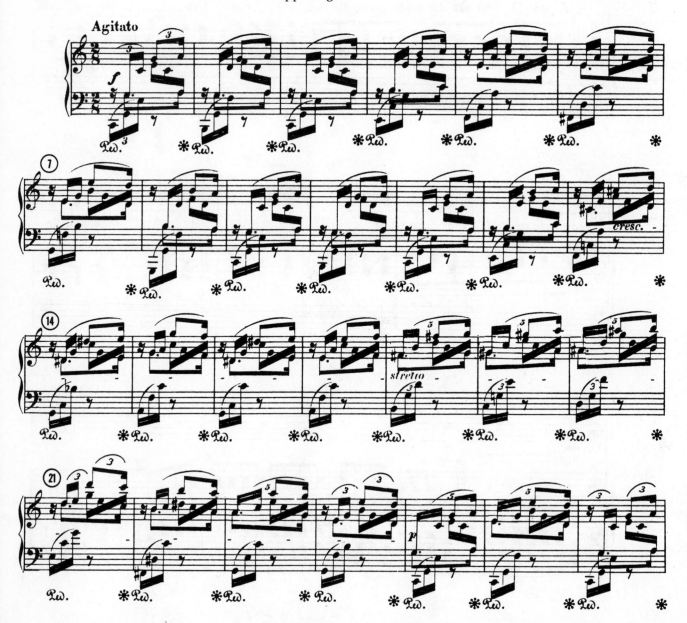

Prelude 2 in A minor

Prelude 4 in E minor

Prelude 6 in B minor

How does the left-hand part serve simultaneously as both principal melody and bass line? What happens at bars 7-8?

Prelude 9 in E major

Prelude 20 in C minor

Prelude 22 in G minor

Why is the chord in bar 5a spelled differently from the chord in bar 17b? Analyze phrases and form.

Six Mazurkas

Frédéric Chopin
(1810–1849)

A Polish folk dance, the mazurka is represented in art music most notably by the mazurkas of Chopin. The six given here exemplify either forms that do not appear elsewhere in this book, or different ways of working out forms that do. They also contain some striking chromaticism.

Mazurka 3 in E major—Op. 6, No. 3

(1830)

Mazurka 5 in B flat major—Op. 7, No. 1

(1830–1831)

Mazurka 24 in C major—Op. 33, No. 3

(1837–1838)

Mazurka 43 in G minor—Op. posth. 67, No. 2

(1849)

Mazurka 45 in A minor—Op. posth. 67, No. 4

(1846)

Mazurka 49 in F minor—Op. posth. 68, No. 4

(1849)

Etude in A flat major

from *Trois Nouvelles Etudes*

(1839)

Frédéric Chopin

(1810–1849)

Because many Chopin etudes have a right-hand part consisting entirely of repetitions of a single short rhythmic pattern, they are sometimes called "one-part" forms. Consider the appropriateness of such a term in the present case. Account for the enharmonicisms at bars 16 and 17 and 26 through 29. The *ossia* in bars 57 through 59 arises from differences in the sources. Which version is musically preferable?

Nocturne in D flat major

Op. 27, No. 2
(1835)

Frédéric Chopin
(1810–1849)

The melodic design and unusual sectional form of this intensely lyrical work might be considered first, then the broad harmonic background and its part in delineating that form. What relation does the key at bars 34 through 37 have to D flat major? Notice the varying degrees of ornateness in the right-hand part: Why are bars 16 and 45, for example, so much more ornate than, say, bar 10, or bars 22 through 25? What is happening in bars 50 through 53?[9]

[9]An analysis of this work is given in Felix Salzer's *Structural Hearing*, Vol. I, p. 251.

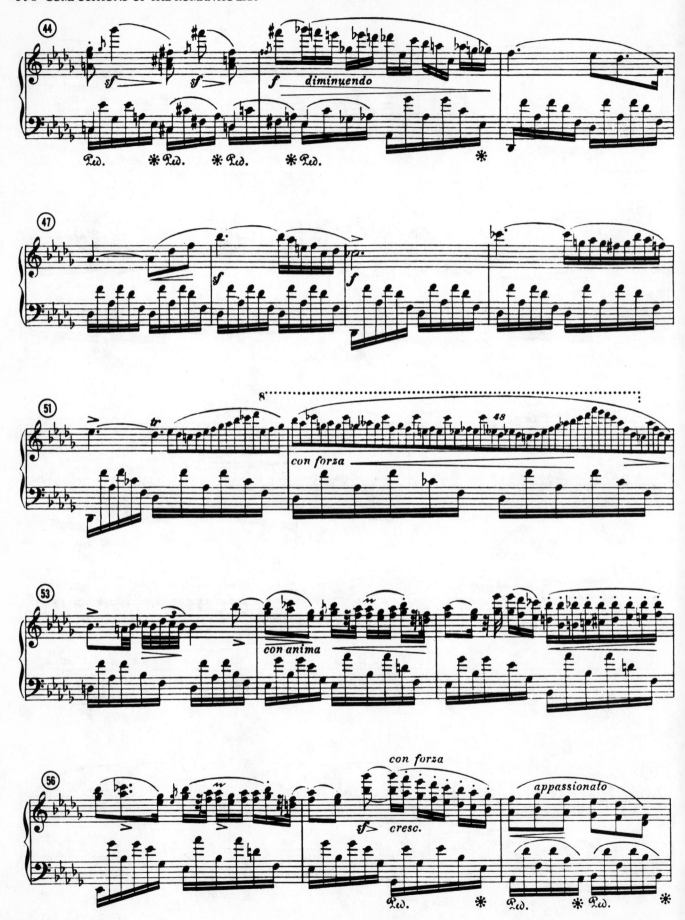

Prelude and Liebestod

from *Tristan and Isolde*

(1857–1859)

Richard Wagner

(1813–1883)

Text: Richard Wagner

in piano-vocal score arranged by Richard Kleinmichel

An eternal problem posed by Wagner's great music drama, *Tristan and Isolde*—and one that has fascinated musicians ever since its creation—is its relation to traditional tonality. Is this music tonal? atonal? a mixture of both? These questions will never be answered to the satisfaction of all, but they inevitably arise in any serious study of the work. In the prelude, for example, can a case be made for a "main" key in spite of the near absence of V-I cadences? In considering this question, notice further that the prelude does not come to a formal conclusion, but ends with a transition to Scene I.[10]

Another aspect of the prelude—and one that is somewhat less elusive than its tonality—is the role of the six interrelated leitmotifs that occur throughout it. The first appearances of these motives are as follows:

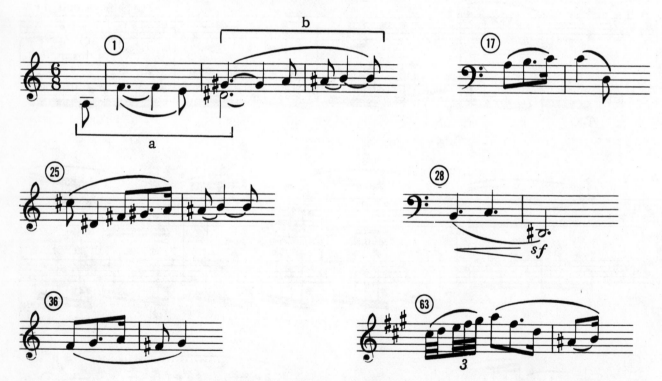

The matter of assigning specific programmatic meanings to the motives is particularly risky in *Tristan*, since this opera is concerned much more with psychological states than with identifiable objects of external reality.[11] However, three

---

[10]The prelude is analyzed in detail in William Mitchell's article, "The Tristan Prelude: Techniques and Structure," in *The Music Forum* (New York: Columbia University Press, 1967), Vol. I, pp. 162–203.

[11]Ernest Newman's *The Wagner Operas* (Knopf, 1949), an excellent introduction to its subject, contains an insightful discussion of the complex question of the leitmotifs in *Tristan*.

of these motives have traditionally been assigned labels that can perhaps be applied without too much over-simplification: No. 1 is called the motive of Desire, or Longing, No. 2 the Look, or Glance, and No. 4 Death. Locate all the occurrences in the prelude of the six motives. How do they contribute to the large, slowly emerging form? Is any one of them dominant? Notice also how two or more statements of a given motive can differ in mood depending on their contexts.

The famous *Liebestod* (Love-Death), which occurs at the very end of the opera, is sung by Isolde after the death of Tristan. At its close she joins Tristan in death. This soaring music contains many passages well worth study: the intensely chromatic voice leading at bars 26 through 29, 38b through 43, and, particularly, 46 through 60; the unusual chromatic sequences at bars 1 through 7, 18 through 25, and 34b through 38; and, of course, one of the most powerful climaxes in music. (At the climax, to what chord does the long-sustained V⁹ immediately progress?) In the *Liebestod*, tonality again poses a problem, though one not as radical as that of the prelude. The key of A flat major appears at the outset, then gives way to an ever-clearer B major as the drama moves toward its close. To appreciate more fully this two-key structure, it is necessary to refer to another well-known portion of the opera, the "Love Duet" of Act II (Schirmer vocal score, pp. 163–195). This much longer portion is likewise founded first on A flat, then on B. As the duet grows in intensity, the Liebestod music is heard for the first time in the opera, but it is not completed here, being interrupted at its highest point. When this music is recapitulated at the very end of the opera— that is, in the Liebestod proper—it *does* reach completion and resolution. What more compelling way to dramatize the idea that the tragic lovers end their longing only in death?

The *Prelude* and the *Liebestod* both contain the Desire motive (No. 1b). Analyze the ambiguous chord that always occurs with the first note (G♯) of this motive, and notice how this chord is each time differently resolved.

A piano arrangement can be of great help in analysis, but the interested student will want to use it together with the full score. For example, see (and hear!) how the Desire motive is frequently characterized by a particular instrumental color.

Prelude

Liebestod

bar 1: Gently, softly,
how he smiles,
how his eyes
he fondly opens!
See ye, friends?
See ye not?
How he shines
ever higher,
soaring on high,
stars sparkling round him?

bar 12: See ye not?
How his heart
proudly swells
and, brave and full,
pulses in his breast?
How softly and gently
from his lips
sweet breath
flutters—
Friends! See!
Do ye not feel and see it?

bar 29: Do I alone
hear the melody
which, so wondrous
and tender
in its sad bliss,
all-revealing,
reconciling,
swelling from him,
pierces me through,
rises higher, [and]
gently sounding,

round me rings?
Yet more clearly,
wafting about me,
are they waves
of gentle breezes?
Are they clouds
of heavenly fragrance?
As they swell
and whisper
shall I breathe them,
shall I listen?
Shall I sip them,
plunge beneath them,
in sweet perfume
breathe out my soul? [and]
in the surging swell,
in the soaring sound,
in the vast wave of
the breath of the world,
drown,
sink down
unconscious—
supreme bliss!

*(Supported by Brangaene,
Isolde, as though
transfigured, gently sinks
onto Tristan's body. Great
emotion among the bystanders.
King Mark blesses the
corpses.)*

*The line starting on G♯ is one octave lower in the score.

Sonata in A major for violin and piano

First Movement (1886)

César Franck (1822–1890)

This movement is a rich example of late nineteenth-century chromaticism. The chromatic motions are frequently best understood in the light of the diatonic progressions that underlie them. Notice also the over-all tonal structure of the movement. Is it in sonata form?

Reprinted from Peters Edition No. 3742. Reprinted permission granted by the publisher, C. F. Peters Corporation, 373 Park Avenue South, New York, N.Y. 10016.

Three Songs

Johannes Brahms
(1833–1897)

The accompaniments of Brahms's songs, far from being mere backgrounds, are unusually rich in motivic life. Frequently they develop motives that appear in the voice part. This is evident to some degree in all three songs given here.

Wiegenlied (Lullaby)—Op. 49, No. 4
(ca. 1868)

Text: Traditional, modified by G. Scherer

The original version of this often-arranged song shows how imaginative an accompaniment can be made of just three well-known chords.

Good evening, good night,
adorned with roses,
bedecked with pinks,
slip under the coverlet.
Tomorrow, if God wills,
thou shalt again awake.

Good evening, good night,
guarded by angels
who will show thee in dreams
the Christ-child's tree.
Sleep sweetly now;
in thy dreams behold Paradise.

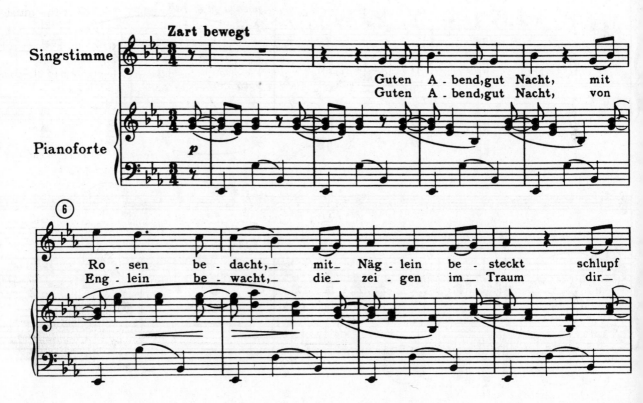

un - ter die Deck: mor - gen früh, wenn Gott will, wirst du wie - der ge -
Christkindleins Baum. Schlaf nun se - lig und süß, schau im Traum's Pa - ra -

weckt, mor - gen früh, wenn Gott will, wirst du wie - der ge - weckt.
dies, schlaf nun se - lig und süß, schau im Traum's Pa - ra - dies.

Minnelied (Love Song)—Op. 71, No. 5

(1877)

Text: Ludwig Hölty

How is the meaning of the text reflected by the music? What is the musical form? How are the voice and piano parts integrated?

Sweeter sing the birds
when the angelic maid
who has conquered my youthful heart
walks through the grove.

Redder bloom the vale and meadow,
greener grows the grass
where the fingers of my lady
gather May flowers.

Without her all is dead,
withered are the plants and blossoms,
and the spring sunset
is no longer clear and fair.

O lovely lady,
may you never flee,
so that my heart, like this meadow,
may bloom in rapture!

Herz, gleich die - ser Au, mög in Won - ne blü - hen, mög in

Won - ne blü - hen!

Feldeinsamkeit (Solitude in the Country)—Op. 86, No. 2

(1877–1878)

Text: Hermann Allmers

Besides the motivic fabric of this atmospheric song, consider as well the musical differences between the settings of the two stanzas.

I rest in silence in the tall green grass,
and long I gaze into the sky above,
surrounded by the crickets' ceaseless song
and wondrously enmeshed in heaven's blue.

I watch the fair and lovely clouds drift on
through the deep blue, like fair and lovely dreams.
It seems as though I have long since been dead,
and with them blissfully drift through eternal space.

Five Intermezzos

Johannes Brahms

(1833–1897)

Brahms contributed much to the Romantic character piece for piano, and gave to many of his compositions in this genre the title "Intermezzo." An important consideration in studying each of the following intermezzos is the way a section or an entire piece will be unified by the repetition of a single motive. Another is the way they reflect the traditional small forms, yet modify those forms by avoiding or veiling the expected.

Intermezzo in B flat major—Op. 76, No. 4

(ca. 1878)

Intermezzo in A major—Op. 118, No. 2

(1893)

Andante teneramente

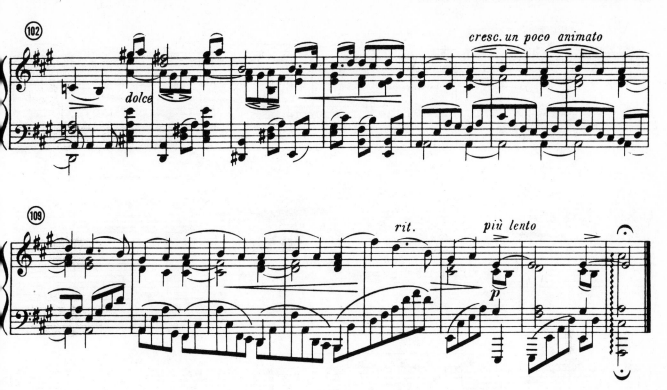

Intermezzo in E flat minor—Op. 118, No. 6.

(1893)

Intermezzo in E minor—Op. 119, No. 2

(1893)

Andantino un poco agitato

Intermezzo in C major—Op. 119, No. 3

(1893)

Three Songs

Hugo Wolf
(1860–1903)

Das verlassene Mägdlein

(1888)

Text: Eduard Mörke

The music of "The Forsaken Maiden" often hints rather than asserts. What is the harmonic background of the first four bars? Where is the first unequivocal statement of the tonic chord? How do the augmented triads fit into the over-all structure?

Early, when the cocks crow,
Before the stars fade out,
I must stand at the hearth,
And light the fire.

Lovely is the flames' light
With its flying sparks;
I gaze into it,
Deep in sorrow.

Suddenly I remember,
Faithless boy,
That I in the night
Of thee have dreamed.

Tear on tear
Tumbles down;
So begins the day—
O, would it were ended!

Schön ist der Flammen Schein, es springen die Fun-ken; ich schaue

so da-rein, in Leid ver - sun - ken.

Plötz-lich, da kommt es mir, treu-lo - ser Kna - be, dass ich die

In dem Schatten meiner Locken

from *Spanisches Liederbuch*

(1889)

Translated from the Spanish by Paul von Heyse and Emanuel Geibel

Progressions in which chord roots lie a third apart play a prominent role in the structure of this song and of *In der Frühe* (page 451). To what extent, if any, does the dominant-tonic relationship still operate in these songs?[12]

In the shadow of my tresses
My beloved has fallen asleep.
Shall I wake him?
Ah no!

With care I comb my curling
Tresses daily at dawn,
But in vain is my toil,
For the winds blow them.
Tresses' shadows and winds' blowing
Have lulled my beloved to sleep.
Shall I wake him?
Ah no!

I must hear how much he grieves,
That he pines so long,
That they give and take from him life—
These my brown cheeks.
And he calls me "Little Viper,"
And yet falls asleep beside me.
Shall I wake him?
Ah no!

12This song is analyzed in part in Felix Salzer's *Structural Hearing*, Vol. II, Graph 382.

In der Frühe

from *Gedichte von Mörike*

(1888)

Text: Eduard Mörike

How are the three stanzas of the text of "In Early Morning" related to the form of the music? How is the meaning of the text expressed by the music?[13] (Also see the remarks before the previous song of Hugo Wolf, p. 446.)

No sleep has cooled my eyes,
And already day appears
At the window of my room.

My troubled mind still tosses
To and fro among doubts
And creates dark phantoms.

Fear and fret no more, my soul!
Be joyful! Already here and yonder
Morning bells are waking.

[13]An analysis of "In der Frühe" is given in Felix Salzer's *Structural Hearing*, Vol. II, Graph 488.

Sehr getragen und schwer

Kein Schlaf noch kühlt das Au - ge mir,

dort ge-het schon der Tag her - für an mei - nem Kam - mer-fen - ster.

Es wüh-let mein ver - stör - ter Sinn noch zwi-schen

PART FIVE

From Debussy to the Present

The compositions in Part Five are intended to represent the mainstream—or main streams—of music in our eventful century. These compositions and some of the basic reasons for choosing them are summarized here, but the sequence in which they are discussed is not necessarily to be taken as the one in which they should be presented to a class. (As with the other parts of this book, teachers will make their own sequence according to their own priorities.) In this summary, the pieces are grouped according to a few very general characteristics. For the most part, each group contains one or more short, sometimes simple, pieces and one larger and/or musically richer piece. Often the smaller can well be studied first by way of working up to the challenges presented by the larger.

It is often difficult to decide the extent to which a twentieth-century work is a manifestation of the traditional tonal system, and, conversely, the exact nature of what the work brings that is new. While one must beware of forcing on a work the familiar norms of the tonal system when they no longer apply, there is no doubt that tonality in the broadest sense governs many twentieth-century works of quite different styles. The basic pitch element in a given work may be a triad, or a triad to which one or more tones are added, or a simultaneity formed of two triads, or a non-triadic chord, an interval, or a single tone. All such constructs other than the traditional triad are loosely referred to by the terms "tonic sonority" or "primary sonority," but their superficial resemblance to the tonic triad in a tonal work should not be overstressed, for the reason that in traditional tonal music the tonic triad brings with it a complete, closed system that operates in essentially the same way at all times—a system, moreover, whose operations are so firmly established that a single note can often imply a number of other notes not explicitly stated; whereas a given "tonic sonority" may function as such in only one work, and must established its own system (assuming it has one) all by itself. Analyzing such a piece can be the discovery of exciting new territory, but understanding it as "tonal" may well obscure its originality. It is sometimes better to explore such music in terms of atonal sets of pitches, but sets assigned to different levels, and perhaps with one pitch or set endowed with highest priority.

Debussy's *Prélude à "L'Après-midi d'un faune,"* though original in many ways, is original largely within the procedures of the triadic tonal system. From a technical standpoint this great work stands alone in Part Five, Debussy's *Feuilles mortes* being much more obviously different from than like it. Ravel's *Le jardin féerique* is also tonal, but is not intended to be specifically related to the Debussy works. Rather, it is interesting for the way it extends the traditional *diatonic* vocabulary, and for its occasional suggestions of modality.

A later type of triadic tonality is represented by the two Hindemith pieces and Bartók's *Bulgarian Rhythm:* Chords of high rank (e.g., final chords of sections) are triads, but chords of subordinate rank are not necessarily so; also, chords of secondary-dominant function are generally (but not always) avoided, though the functional dominant still occurs as an element of high structural rank. Study of Hindemith's *A Swan* might well precede analysis of the movement from his second piano sonata.

The pieces comprising the next group are particularly problematic because, while triads are prominent on their surface, harmonic functionality and traditional voice-leading techniques are either absent or highly modified. This group as a whole might broadly be characterized as based on sonorities of either the "added-tone" or "polytriad" type. An added-tone chord consists of one triad to which one or more tones is added (e.g., the "chord of the added sixth"). In analyzing such chords, one must frequently ask whether the added tones themselves differ in rank or function from the tones of the triad. That is, do they merely color the triad, or do they have a more organic function? A polytriad is composed of two, sometimes three, distinct, often registrally separated, triads (or seventh chords). In analyzing polytriadic pieces or passages, one often cannot apply the tonal concepts of *root* or *bass;* rather, one must frequently look to melodic events in the upper register for the determining factors.

On its surface, Charles Ives's *General William Booth Enters into Heaven* is extraordinarily rich in clear examples of both added-tone chords and polytriads as well as many other twentieth-century innovations in both pitch and rhythm. While traditional functionality is certainly not absent, an overall view of the work must take into account a recurring added-tone sonority of high rank. The short movement from Schuman's *Three-Score Set* is suitable for an initial presentation of polytriads; it can well be followed by Bartók's *Syncopation* and Stravinsky's *March* from *L'histoire du soldat.* All three of these pieces are surpassed in scope and content by the excerpt from Stravinsky's *Le sacre du printemps,* which, in spite of its being only a section (the only one in the book), is well worth detailed study. Though Stravinsky's *Theme with Variations* is offered primarily for the analysis of its serial aspect (see below), it is relevant here for its use of purely *diatonic* added-tone chords (see end of Theme) and polytriads (see especially Variation 1).

At some point it becomes imperative to postulate the twelve tones of the tempered chromatic scale as the basic precompositional material. In presenting this concept to students, a traditional—and still viable—method has been to relate it at once to twelve-tone *serialism.* However, the great development in atonal theory of the last several decades has extensively widened the understanding of the properties of this precompositional material, and sees serialism as just one (though a very significant) manifestation of it. And it has also greatly widened the repertory of works that can be fruitfully examined in "twelve-tone" terms. Therefore, an alternative teaching method would be to introduce to students some of the basic properties of the twelve-tone material before concentrating on serialism. Chief among these is its "regularity"—that is, its construction by means of a single (and therefore regularly recurring) interval, the half step, as opposed to the "irregular" construction of the tonal system's diatonic scale. From this property flows the partitionability of the octave into intervals of equal size, e.g., six whole steps, four minor thirds, etc. In composition, it is regularity that makes possible *real*, as opposed to *tonal*, motivic transposition and—more significantly—*real inversion*, a phenomenon frequently discussed in terms of two "symmetrical" formations lying equidistant above and below an "axis of symmetry." Real inversion scarcely exists in pre-twentieth-century music, and when it does it is either fortuitous or a compositional *tour de force* (like the remarkable Bach canon, *Quaerendo invenietis*, given on page 141). It never exists on the level of harmonic structure, since triads in the tonal system are generated only from the bottom up, not from a center *out*. A tonal melody such as, for example, the subject of *The Art of the Fugue*, may be tonally inverted to read A-D-F-A-B ♭-A-G-F, but this inversion, just like the upright form, is founded on the D-rooted triad, D-F-A. To put the matter another way: Subjecting the tonic triad D-F-A to *real* inversion from the axis D produces a descending D-B-G, a formation which, *as far as D minor is concerned*, is simply another right-side-up triad, namely, the IV ♮3 chord. In tonal theory there is no need for recognition of the fact that D-B-G is the real inversion of D-F-A. Precisely the reverse is true in atonal theory, in which real invertibility is axiomatic.

In this anthology a group of pieces by Bartók and Scriabin clearly isolates real inversion and shows its application in a number of very different but relatively simple ways. The simplest is "mirror writing" of the most obvious type—that is, as used in Bartók's *Bulgarian Rhythm*, bars 18 and 19. This charming (and earlier mentioned) piece is structurally interesting because of its use of real inversion *within* triadic tonality: Its extensive symmetries are ultimately subordinated to the G-major triad. The rest of the pieces in the group are atonal; if they contain any tonal elements, these are subordinated to inversional organization. The simplest such piece is Bartók's *Diminished Fifth*, in which the various tetrachords played by one hand are continually reflected inversionally in the other hand, with free permutation within each tetrachord. This little piece may also serve to introduce the inherently symmetrical "octatonic" scale.[1] In the more complex and musically richer *Minor Seconds, Major Sevenths* of Bartók, the primary sonority E ♭-G ♯-A-D (note the relation to the octatonic scale) and several transpositions thereof are treated in turn to imaginative elaborations, some of which proceed symmetrically, some not. Neither of the two pieces from Scriabin's *Five Preludes*, Op. 74, makes use of symmetry, but the "regularity" of the material is here exploited on the highest level in that the structure of both pieces is founded on the space of an octave partitioned into intervals of equal size. Finally, symmetry on the structural level (not on the note-to-note level) is exemplified in the fugue from Bartók's *Music for Strings, Percussion, and Celesta*, the scope and artistic merit of which far transcend that of the other pieces in this group. Here the single tone a[1] is the primary axis of symmetry. Such an axis is not necessarily also a "tonic sonority," but in this case a[1] is that as well.

"Free" atonality is a term used to characterize the post-tonal, pre-dodecaphonic repertory of Schoenberg and his school—an extremely varied body of works the understanding of which has been greatly promoted by recent advances in theory. The shortest such work in the anthology is the fourth of

---

[1]The octatonic scale is formed of alternating whole and half steps, e.g., E ♭-F-G ♭-A ♭-A-B-C-D. It was first(?) used by Rimsky-Korsakoff, who explicitly described it in *My Musical Life* (English translation: Knopf, New York, 1923), p. 72. The relevance of this scale to the analysis of music by various early twentieth-century composers has only recently been realized. See especially Arthur Berger's "Problems of Pitch Organization in Stravinsky," in *Perspectives of New Music*, (Fall-Winter, 1963), particularly p. 20f. See also Pieter van den Toorn's "Some Characteristics of Stravinsky's Diatonic Music," in the same journal, (Fall-Winter, 1975), p. 104f.

[2]Since there is no universally used twelve-tone terminology, one consistent set of terms had to be selected for the comments on the twelve-tone pieces. The few terms used here originated with Milton Babbitt. Definitions will be found in George Perle's *Serial Composition and Atonality* (Berkeley and Los Angeles: University of California Press, 1977, 4th ed), pp. 2–4; p. 156.

Webern's *Five Movements for String Quartet*, Op. 5. Study of this piece can precede that of Schoenberg's very rewarding piano piece, Op. 11, No. 1. In a class by itself is Schoenberg's famous orchestral piece, here called by its English name, *Summer Morning by a Lake (Colors)*. While the most important dimension of this piece is indeed its color, its pitch organization is also of great interest, featuring as it does a five-note primary sonority. In a world apart is Charles Ives's song, *The Cage*, an example of American "free atonality." And Debussy's *Feuilles mortes*, though included chiefly to show some of the more obvious surface aspects of the composer's late style, has a structure that might be more fruitfully explored from an atonal rather than a tonal point of view.

Serialism in a non-dodecaphonic framework is exemplified by Stravinsky's *Theme with Variations*, wherein the theme is subjected to free rhythmic alteration, change of register, and note repetition in the manner of a tone row. Twelve-tone serialism is represented by six pieces quite consciously chosen to proceed from simple to complex and to reveal a variety of procedures. The movement from Krenek's *Suite* for solo cello uses only one set-form; Dallapiccola's expressive *Quartina* shows all four aspects of the set, set transposition, and one way in which two set-forms can be combined. Webern's song, *Wie bin ich froh!*, makes significant compositional use of pitch duplications between inversionally complementary set-forms, and his *Variations for Piano*, second movement, is a more complex demonstration of the same principle. A very different approach to twelve-tone composition is exemplified by Schoenberg's song, *Sommermüd*, which displays the row segmented into subsets, with free permutation and repetition within the subsets. The first of Milton Babbitt's *Three Compositions for Piano* exploits the combinatorial property of its twelve-tone set, and also serializes rhythm.

Not all the selections in Part Five were made on the basis of pitch organization. The dimension of color was a deciding factor not only in the Schoenberg orchestral piece, as noted, but also in Elliott Carter's one-note etude for woodwind quartet. Henry Cowell's *The Banshee* was chosen for its very untraditional approach to sound production (and for fun).

New ways of treating rhythm has also been a factor in selecting certain pieces, notably the excerpt from Stravinsky's *Le sacre*, Bartók's *Syncopation*, and especially Elliott Carter's brilliant study in metrical modulation—the *Canaries* for solo tympani. Unmetered rhythm is found in Ives's *The Cage* and in the madrigal of George Crumb. The latter work and Bruce Saylor's *Psalm 13* take different approaches to the notation of rhythm, but both approaches are typical of much recent music. The Saylor piece also introduces elements of chance into the domains of both rhythm and pitch.

One final criterion has influenced certain choices—the persistence of certain ancient forms and genres (or at least their wraiths) into modern times. The General Index cites such examples of simple binary and ternary forms, sonata form, variations, fugue, canon, and rondo.

Prélude à "L'Aprés-midi d'un faune"

(1892–1894)

Claude Debussy

(1862–1918)

Piano arrangement: Ladislas Kun

Debussy's evocative masterpiece, *Prelude to "The Afternoon of a Faun,"* is scored for three flutes, two oboes, English horn, two clarinets, two bassoons, four horns, antique cymbals turned to e^2 and b^2, two harps, and strings. We give it in piano reduction to facilitate analysis, mindful that many details can be fully perceived only by recourse to the full score.

Notice the numerous transformations of the opening theme that appear throughout the work. It is also instructive to reduce a portion of the work, such as bars 1 through 30, to its essential voice leading. Do chords progress in traditional fashion? What is the function of the whole-tone material in bars 31—36, 48—50, 58, and 92? Does dominant-tonic functionality exist in this work? What aspects of the work were unprecedented at the time of composition?[3]

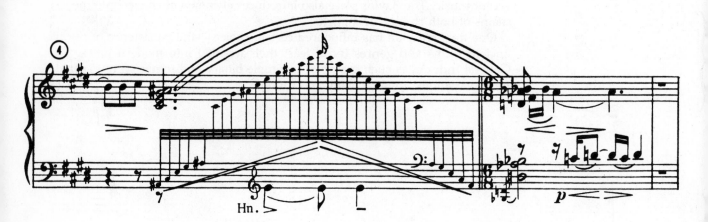

[3]The first large section is analyzed by Felix Salzer in his *Structural Hearing*. Vol. II, Graph 455. Analytic comment on the entire work is given on pp. 69–96 of *Debussy: Prelude to "The Afternoon of a Faun,"* edited by William W. Austin, in the Norton Critical Scores series (New York: W. W. Norton & Company, 1970).

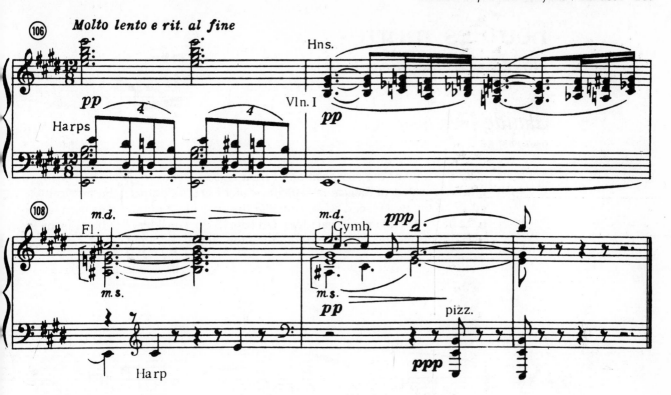

Feuilles mortes

No. 2 of *Préludes, Book II*
(1910–1913)

Claude Debussy
(1862–1918)

By the time of the composition of *Dead Leaves*, Debussy's style had changed much from that of *Prelude to "Afternoon of a Faun."* Compare the musical language of the two pieces. Also, consider the later piece purely in its own terms; trace the course of its musical ideas. (At bars 25–30, consider possible reasons for the curious spelling of the chords in the top staff.)

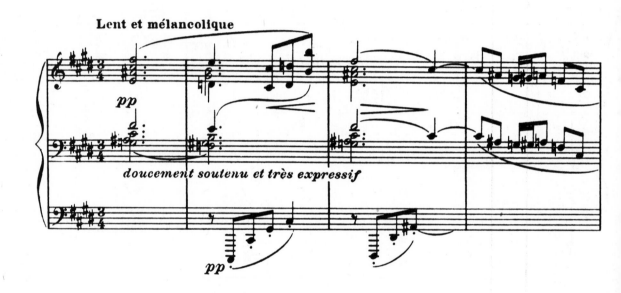

Un peu plus allant et plus gravement expressif

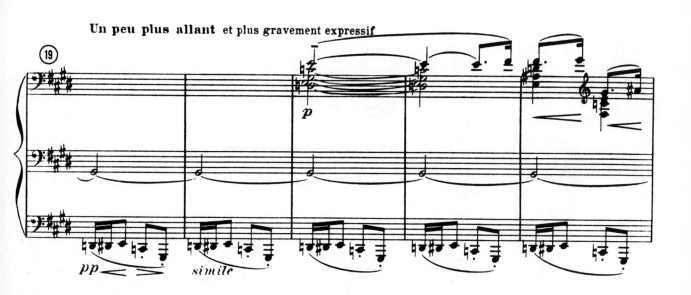

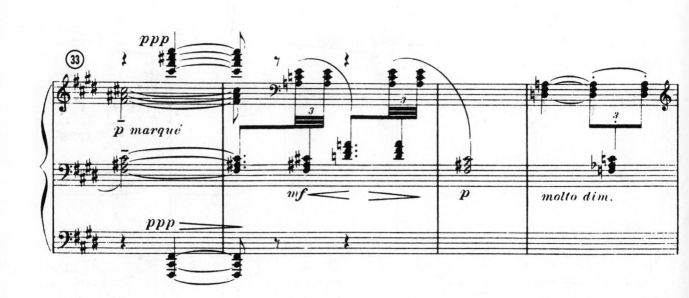

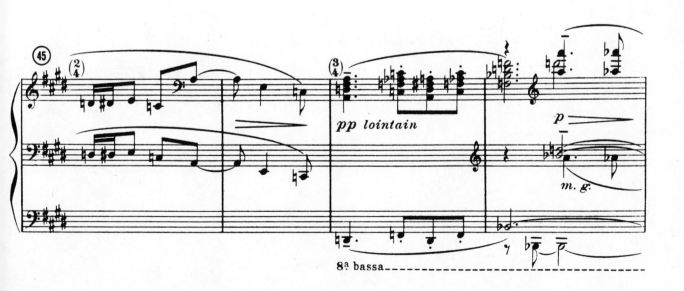

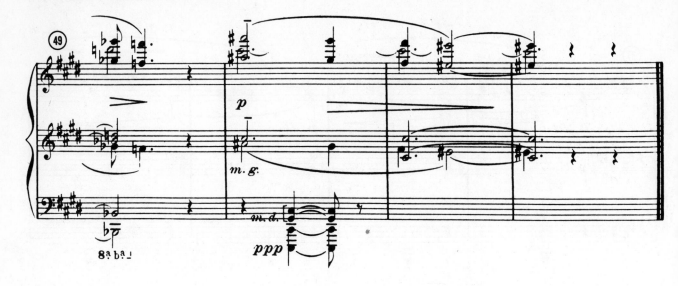

Two Preludes

from *Five Preludes*, Op. 74
(1914)

Alexander Scriabin
(1872–1915)

This century has seen many attempts to develop musical systems on axioms other than the diatonic scale and the I–V relationship. Some of the works of Alexander Scriabin, including Op. 74, his last composition, provide remarkable early examples. *Prelude No. 3* is the simpler of the two quoted here and should be examined first. Its basic pitch material is a set of eight tones explicitly stated in scalar form in the right-hand part of bar 12. Examine the properties of this octatonic scale and the piece that is here made of it, which adheres strictly to the notes of the scale (except for a few short, rhythmically weak passing tones such as the g$\sharp^1$ in bar 1).

The hyperemotional first prelude is also basically octatonic. Its scale may be deduced from the chords falling on the first beat of every bar except bars 5 and 6, where a "modulation" to another octatonic scale occurs. (No distinction is made between enharmonically spelled notes.) However, there are more non-scalar tones here than in Prelude 3—including the last note struck. Scalar content aside, it will prove valuable to analyze the over-all structure of the work.

The construction of the chords favored by Scriabin in both the preludes should also be noticed. Have the chords any antecedents in traditional harmony? What is the nature of "chord progression" in this music?

Though the octatonic scale is too limited—like the whole-tone scale—to furnish the basis of large compositions, it figures in passages and short pieces by many composers. An example by Bartók will be found on page 512. Compare the harmonies Bartók makes from the scale with those in the Scriabin pieces. What other chords does the scale yield?

Op. 74, No. 1

Douloureux déchirant

Op. 74, No. 3

Allegro drammatico

No. 1 of *Three Piano Pieces*, Op. 11

(1909; revised 1942)

Arnold Schoenberg

(1874–1951)

This composition is one of Schoenberg's earliest atonal works. Once the object of protest and violent controversy, it can today be heard for what it is—a powerful and expressive piece of late Romantic music. It should be performed with very clear projection of the crescendo and diminuendo marks, and with a degree of rubato.

First, play or hear the piece repeatedly, and discover its motives, themes, and large sections. Listen in particular for recurrences of materials presented in the first 13 bars. They are frequently somewhat modified in repetition, but still retain their basic shape and are quite recognizable. For example, what is being repeated in bars 34 and 35?

Then listen for finer details of pitch organization. Notice especially the intervallic content of the first three notes b^1-$g\sharp^1$-$g\natural^1$, and how this set of notes is subsequently treated to various operations (such as transpositions, change of register, verticalization, inversion, retrograde, etc.). For example, see in bars 4 and 5 the G$\sharp$-b-g^1; see also bar 10 (right hand only), and bar 12's first 4 notes, and bar 19—and many more places. (But do not look for a *twelve*-tone set; Schoenberg was still years from that concept.) While this three-note set is a very important one in the piece, there are other, related, sets that are also quite prominent. But not every note in the piece can be understood as a member of a set—only quite a few.[4] (Another well-known, and shorter, atonal work, the fourth of Webern's *Five Pieces for String Quartet*, Op. 5, is given on page 548.)

Drei *Klavierstücke*, op. 11, No. 1, by Schoenberg. Copyright 1910 by Universal Edition; Renewed 1938 by Arnold Schoenberg. Used by permission of Belmont Music Publishers, Los Angeles, California 90049; and used by permission of European American Music Distributors Corp.

[4]George Perle gives extensive analytic comment on this movement in his *Serial Composition and Atonality* (Berkeley and Los Angeles: University of California Press, 4th ed., 1977), p. 10ff.

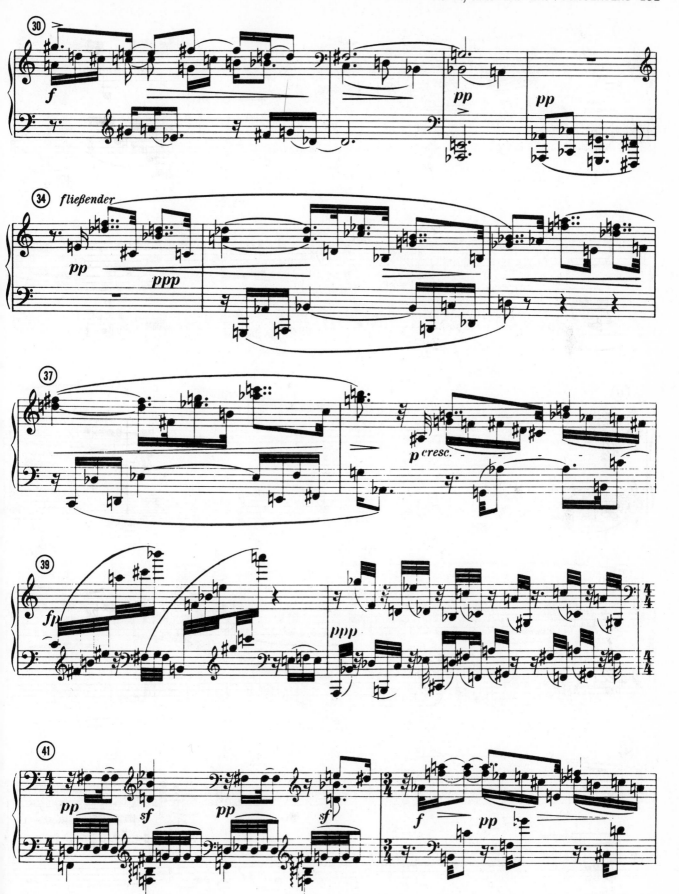

Sommermorgen an einem See—Summer Morning by a Lake
(Farben)   (Colors)

ARNOLD SCHOENBERG

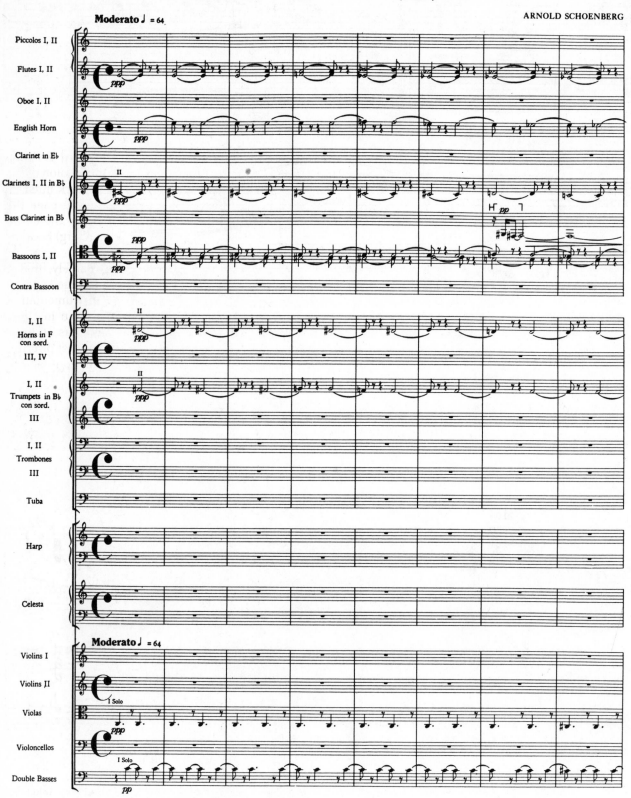

The change of chords in this piece has to be executed with the greatest subtlety, avoiding accentuation of entering instruments, so that only the difference in color becomes noticeable.
The conductor need not try to polish sounds which seem unbalanced, but watch that every instrumentalist plays accurately the prescribed dynamic, according to the nature of his instrument. There are no motifs in this piece which have to be brought to the fore.

Summer Morning by a Lake (Colors)

No. 3 of *Five Pieces for Orchestra,* Op. 16

(1909)

Arnold Schoenberg

(1874–1951)

Arrangement for two pianos: Anton Webern (1913)

The idea for this composition, Schoenberg's famous experiment in "tone color melody" (*Klangfarbenmelodie*), came to him from an actual impression of the colors of the sunrise reflected in the waters of a lake. Since the work must be understood first of all in terms of color, we show on the preceding page the beginning of the orchestral score (in the 1949 revision); but we give the entire piece in a piano arrangement (made by a noted student of Schoenberg) because it facilitates enormously the study of this fascinating work.

This piece was long the victim of a popular misconception, namely, that it consisted of but a single chord, sustained from start to end that changed only in its color, that is, in its instrumentation. While it is true that the instrumentation does so change, there is much more to the pitch organization than just one chord. Perceptive listening will also reveal that, though this piece has no tonic *triad,* the chord that both opens and closes it is obviously of the highest priority. What happens to this chord—*besides* the changes in instrumentation—as the work progresses?[5]

#3 "Farben" from *Five Pieces for Orchestra* by Arnold Schoenberg, edited for 2 pianos by Anton von Webern. Copyright 1913 by C. F. Peters Corporation, 373 Park Avenue South, New York, New York 10016. Copyright renewed 1941 by C. F. Peters Corporation. Permission granted by the publisher.

[5]This work is discussed in my article, "Schoenberg's *Farben*," *Perspectives of New Music*, (Fall–Winter 1973), p. 141. A short piece founded exclusively on the principle of *Klangfarbenmelodie* is given on page 574 of this anthology, and a very different experiment in color on page 564.

Sommermüd

No. 1 of *Three Songs*, Op. 48

(1933)

Arnold Schoenberg

(1874–1951)

Text: Jakob Haringer

> When life seems an endless night,
> Suddenly an evening will again bring kisses and stars.
>
> When everything seems over,
> Once again it will be Christmas Eve or lovely May.
>
> So be still and thank God you still live and kiss:
> For many without a star have had to die.

The way Schoenberg handles the twelve-tone system in *Summer Weariness* is very typical of his style. It should be compared with Webern's very different approach to the twelve-tone system as shown in his song, *Wie bin ich froh!* (page 551).

Consider the first eight pitches of the voice part to be order-numbers 1 through 8 of P–0, and notice how they divide musically as 4 + 4. Encircle both of these four-note subsets and call them A and B, respectively. The remaining four-note subset, C, occurs in bars 1 through 3 as the piano part, but is here treated in such a way that it is impossible to determine the order of its pitch classes. To find the pitch order of subset C, look for the recurrence of P–0 later in the song. R, I, and RI forms of the set also occur in the course of the composition. Like P–0 at the beginning, each is typically segmented as 4 + 4 + 4 (though a slightly different sort of segmentation occurs at bars 10 and 11). Figure out all the set-forms in the composition. When a given set-form has been identified, it is not always necessary to place an order number beside *every* pitch; often it will suffice simply to encircle each of the three four-note segments and identify them as A, B, and C.

Besides merely figuring out the twelve-tone sets (a necessary first step), consider also how the set and its treatment are related to the poem. In this regard, notice how certain pitches in the song stand out to create quite audible long-range connections. What "form" is discernible in this composition?

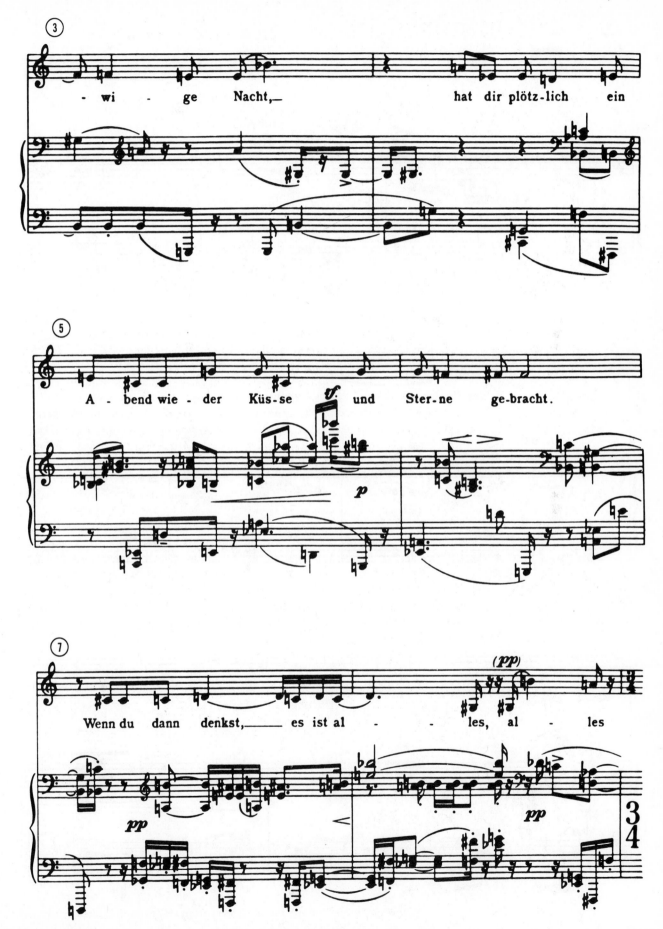

The Cage

No. 64 of *114 Songs*
(1906)

Charles Ives
(1874–1954)

Text: Charles Ives

The American Ives, whose astonishingly early experiments with new compositional materials frequently preceded their use by then better-known European composers, has here set a vocal line to a piano part that conflicts with it in many ways. Consider the relation of these conflicting elements both in purely musical terms and in light of the meaning of the text. The absence of meter and bar lines in no way contradicts Ives's demand for a precisely measured performance. Figure out the rhythm of the first seven chords until you can play it (or tap it out) with absolute accuracy.[6]

[6]The version of *The Cage* given here is essentially that given in the *114 Songs*, which Ives printed at his own expense in 1922. The music also exists in two other versions, both published as part of *A Set of Pieces for Theatre or Chamber Orchestra* in *New Music* (San Francisco: Pacific Music Press, January, 1932, Vol. 5, No. 2). Since the later versions are notated with more rhythmic precision, a few rhythmic details therefrom have been incorporated in the version given here. The other versions also clarify the second chord in the second system: It is correctly written as dotted half notes and should be held by the pedal through the following chord. All pitches here are exactly as given in *114 Songs*.

back to the oth - er side; he stopped on - ly when the keep - er came a - round with meat;

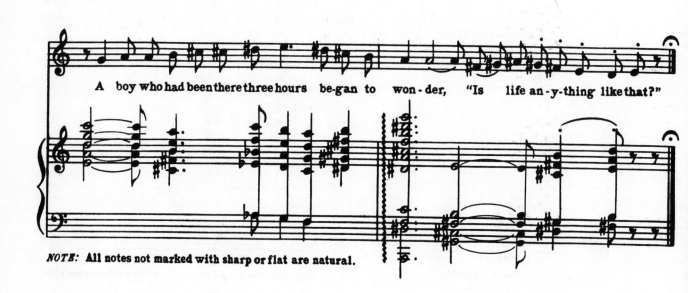

A boy who had been there three hours be-gan to won-der, "Is life an-y-thing like that?"

NOTE: All notes not marked with sharp or flat are natural.

General William Booth Enters into Heaven

(1914)

Charles Ives

(1874–1954)

Text: Lines 1–23 and 30–37 of Vachel Lindsay's poem of the same name.

Growing up in a small New England town, the young Charles Ives, son of the local bandmaster, soaked up the many and varied popular songs that were part of the common culture: patriotic songs, marches, minstrel songs, hymns, gospel songs, folk songs. He absorbed these early influences so thoroughly that many such tunes, or something like them, quite naturally appeared later in his compositions, but now transformed—part of something of a higher order.

The musical quotations in *General William Booth Enters into Heaven* are chiefly from the gospel song *Fountain* (or *Western Melody*), which Ives must have heard many times at the camp meetings of his boyhood. This song appears as follows in *Gospel Hymns*, published by Biglow & Main, New York, 1883:

Ives also quotes briefly from two other popular melodies: The first, quoted at bars 52 through 55 (piano part), is the minstrel song *Golden Slippers* by James A. Bland; the other at bars 70 through 73, is too well-known to need identification here.

The student of this music will want to analyze the relation of the gospel tune to Ives's composition. But there is much more in *General Booth*. The song is a virtual compendium of the innovations in harmony and rhythm that characterized much early twentieth-century music. These sometimes take the form of great washes of sound that tax the ten fingers of the human hand, but for all this the composition is actually quite tightly constructed, wholly convincing both in its large gestures and its details.

The words of *Fountain* are not used in Ives's song, which uses only Vachel Lindsay's poem. (Lindsay also quotes from a gospel song, *Are You Washed in the Blood of the Lamb?*, but Ives did not make use of the tune of this song.) Listeners sometimes take the poem to be satiric, but it is first of all a tribute to William Booth, founder of the Salvation Army, whose uninhibited "soldiers" waged their battles in squalid slums and prisons to save society's lowest outcasts. If the poem has satire, it is an implied satire of the attitudes of "respectable" society with its comfortable, official religion. Ives's music is a perfect match. It is full of color and high spirits, but, like the poem, makes a quite serious point.[7]

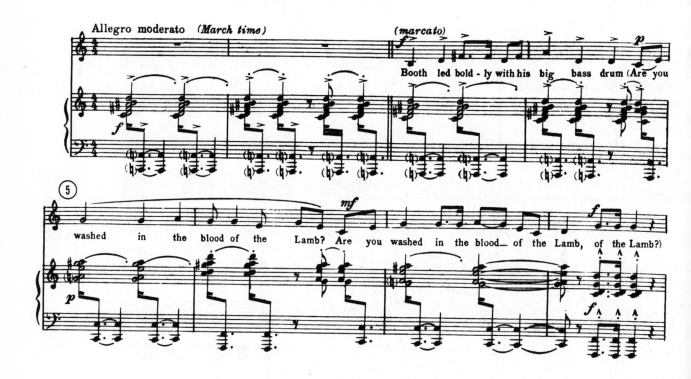

General William Booth Enters into Heaven, by Ives. Copyright 1935 by Merion Music, Inc. Used by permission.

Words reprinted with permission of Macmillan Publishing Co., Inc., from *Collected Poems* of Vachel Lindsay.

[7]General Booth was also arranged for solo voice, chorus, and orchestra. The small notes in the score given here refer to the chorus part of that arrangement.

Le jardin féerique

No. 5 from *Ma mère l'Oye*

(1908)

Maurice Ravel

(1875–1937)

The *Mother Goose* suite—a work typical of Ravel's vision of the magical world of the child—was originally composed for piano, 4 hands, but later orchestrated by the composer. *The Enchanted Garden*, which closes the suite, is given here in a *two*-hand piano arrangement by Jacques Charlot. Study of its harmony and form will reveal some of the ways that Ravel extended the traditional diatonic vocabulary. To what extent, if any, can one find here scales other than major and minor? Analyze the chords that constitute the final cadence.

arpéger le moins possible

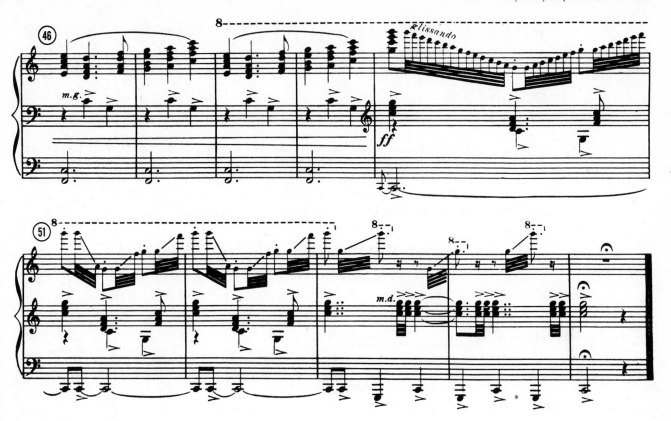

Four Pieces from *Mikrokosmos*
(1926–1937)

Béla Bartók
(1881–1945)

Mikrokosmos ("the universe in small"), a series of 153 short piano pieces that grow progressively more difficult, is, in addition to its great value to the student of piano-playing, a rich compendium of compositional materials and techniques that displays the many facets of the composer's work. This selection emphasizes some of the most typical and basic of these facets.

Bulgarian Rhythm (No. 115, Vol. IV)

What gives direction to the pitches of this little piece?

[23 sec.]

Syncopation (No. 133, Vol. V)

How is the effect of syncopation created in this piece? That is, why would a listener who had never seen the score hear the rhythm as syncopated? Could one just as readily hear the eighth notes in bar 1 as 123 1234 123? Or as 123 123 12 12? (See also the questions pertaining to rhythm in the comments on the Bartók orchestral work given on page 517.) Aside from questions of rhythm what gives coherence and direction to the organization of the pitches?

[1 min. 5 sec.]

Diminished Fifth (No. 101, Vol. IV)

What scale is used in this composition?

Minor Seconds, Major Sevenths (No. 144, Vol. VI)

This is one of Bartók's numerous compositions that seems to evoke the mysteriousness of the night with its blurred images and sounds. What is the basis of its pitch organization? What is the function of the elaborate tempo changes?

[3 min. 25 sec.]

Music for String Instruments, Percussion, and Celesta

First Movement

(1936)

Béla Bartók

(1881–1945)

The fugue is an ancient musical form that has had a new lease on life in the twentieth century. In this famous example (which opens a four-movement work), subject and episode are readily located. But a more interesting aspect of this fugue is its over-all "tonal" plan, which is a unique fusion of old and new. One way to begin exploring it is to make a diagram showing the pitch level of each statement of the subject. How does the powerful climax fit into the over-all plan?

The rhythm of this fugue suggests another kind of question. Notice that many of its bars are divided into unequal parts (shown by dotted lines). See, for example, bar 19, which has a 3 + 3 + 2 grouping. Now turn to the Bartók piece starting on page 510 compare its second bar, which is likewise 3 + 3 + 2. Ignoring the difference in tempo, consider how these two passages differ in their basic rhythmic effect.

Another twentieth-century fugue is given on page 544.

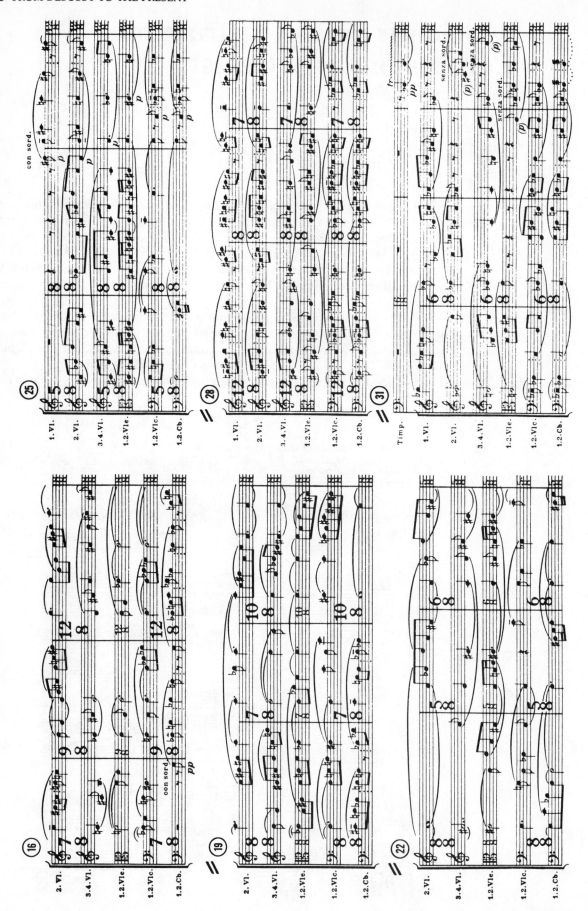

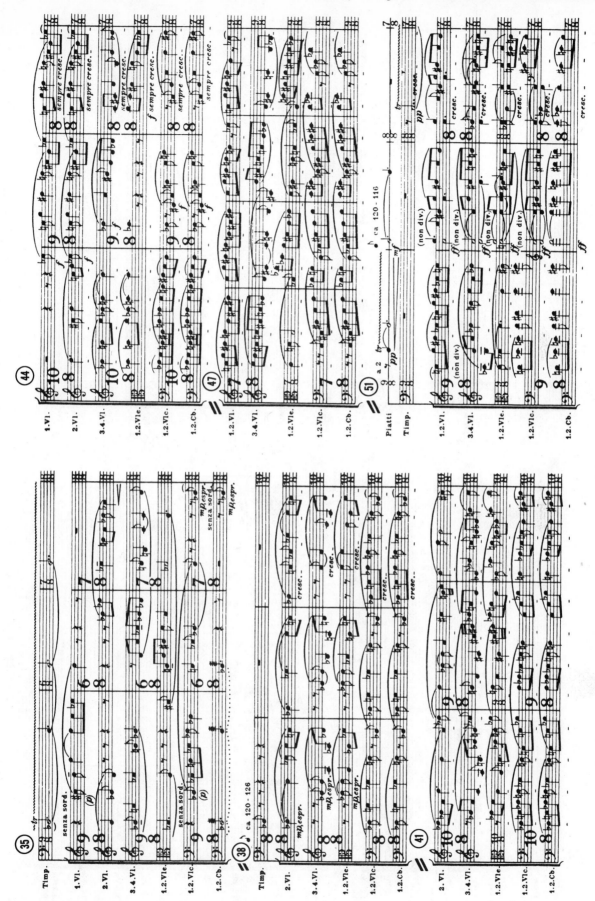

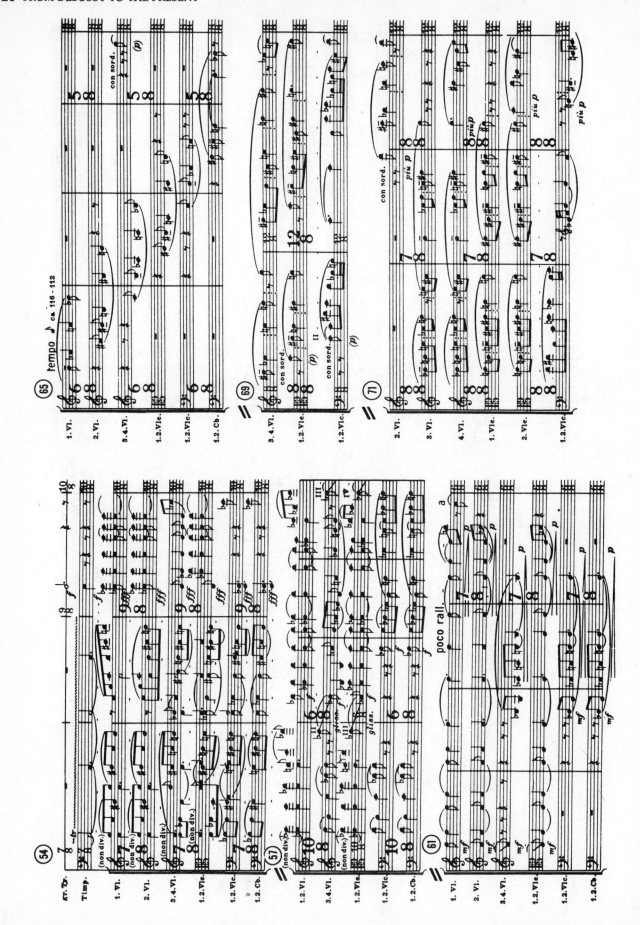

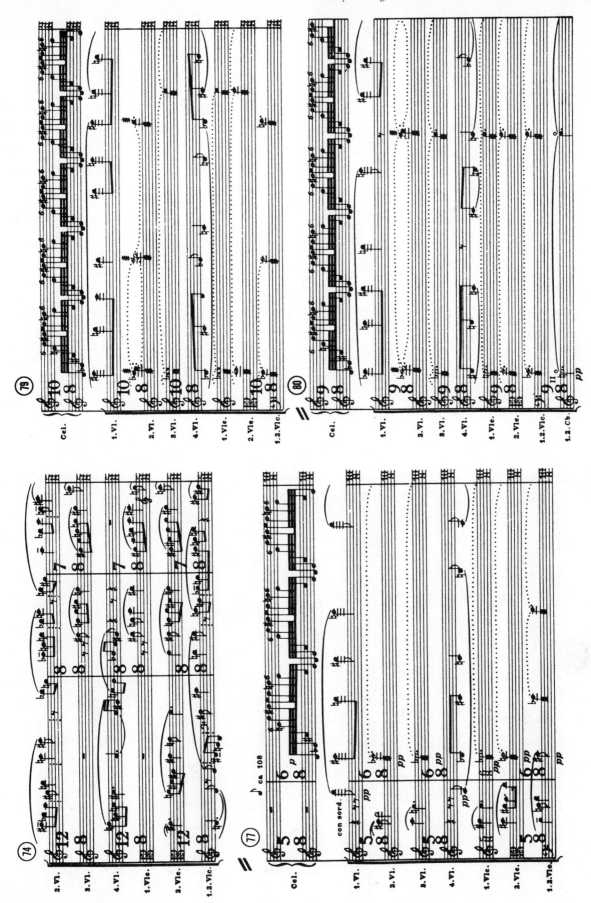

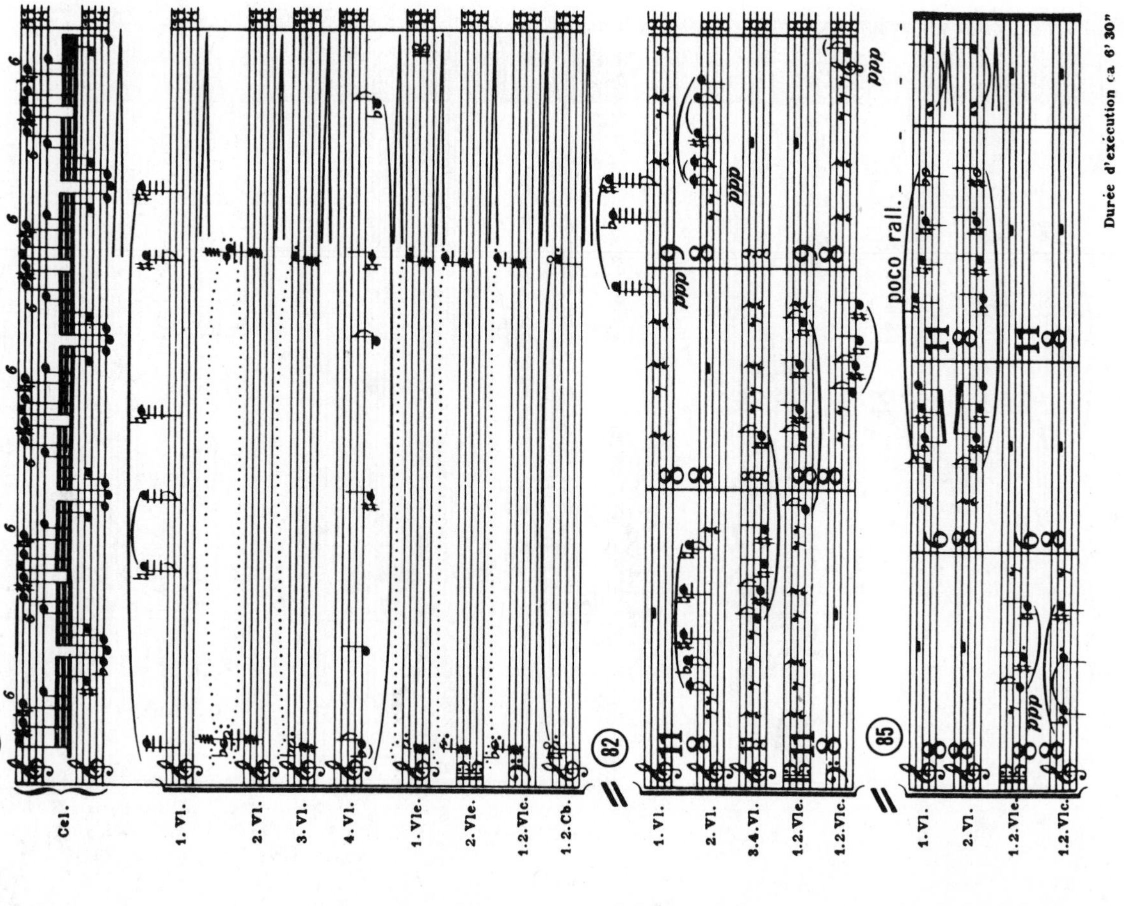
81
Cel.
1. Vl.
2. Vl.
3. Vl.
4. Vl.
1. Vle.
2. Vle.
1.2. Vlc.
1.2. Cb.
82
1. Vl.
2. Vl.
3.4. Vl.
1.2. Vle.
1.2. Vlc.
ppp
85
1. Vl.
2. Vl.
1.2. Vle.
1.2. Vlc.
poco rall.
Durée d'exécution ca 6' 30"

Le Sacre du printemps

Introduction to Part II

(1911–1912)

Igor Stravinsky

(1882–1971)

Arrangement for piano, four hands, by the composer

Throughout much of his long life, Stravinsky sought to fashion new combinations out of materials inherited from the past. In addition to the important differences in style and technique between the three selections from his music given below, what specific similarities do some or all of them have?

The introduction to the second of the two parts of *The Rite of Spring* depicts the night prior to the ritual sacrifice of the chosen maiden. It leads without pause into the next section, "Mysterious Circles of the Adolescents," the beginning of which also has been included here (bars 56–63).

In the first bar, the left hand of the *prima* part consists wholly of minor triads. How do these triads relate to the chord in the *seconda* part? Trace the evolution of the melodic idea first announced in bar 9 (*prima*, right hand). Analyze the conduct of the several ostinatos that gradually emerge between bars 27 and 47. How are they distinguished one from the other? How are they related harmonically?[8]

Useful as piano reductions are, they are, of course, subordinate to the full score. Space forbids giving both in their entirety, but on the next page we show bars 6 through 11 of the score (original version). By comparing the two, much can be learned about orchestration, reduction—and *The Rite of Spring*.

Piano reduction continued on p. 525.

[8]Detailed analytic comment on *Le Sacre du printemps*, especially on its rhythmic organization, is given by Pierre Boulez in his *Notes of an Apprenticeship*, trans. by Herbert Weinstock (New York: Alfred A. Knopf, 1968). The opening of Part II is discussed on pages 75–79 and 99–105.

**CERCLES MYSTERIEUX
DES ADOLESCENTES**

Marche du Soldat

from *L'Histoire du soldat*

(1918)

Igor Stravinsky

(1882–1971)

Arrangement for piano by the composer

Text: C. F. Ramuz
English version: Michael Flanders and Kitty Black

One readily observed dimension of this witty take-off on the conventions of the march is its mosaic of related motives. Distinguish between them, and analyze their development. More elusive are the harmonic and tonal aspects of the composition. Examine the simultaneously associated traids; does any one tone, triad, or polytriad have priority in the structure of the movement as a whole?

This march frequently subverts the listener's rhythmic expectations. How do the $\frac{3}{8}$ bars fit into a piece that is basically in $\frac{2}{4}$ time? Does the final chord *sound* like a strong or weak beat?

L'Histoire du soldat is scored for clarinet in A, bassoon, cornet in A, trombone, percussion, violin, and contrabass. We have chosen to give this piano arrangement, which is very close to the original, in order to facilitate analysis. Indications of instruments have been added, and a few misprints corrected.[9]

Reprinted by permission of J. & W. Chester/Edition Wilhelm Hansen London Ltd

[9]The fifths g^1-d^2 starting in bar 64 are an octave lower in the score, where they are assigned to the violin. In bars 69–70 of the arrangement the original octave is used. The fifths a^1-e^2 that start in bar 71 and continue through bar 83 are peculiar to this arrangement. In the score this is a continuation of the violin fifths g–d^1 begun in bar 64. The problem could have been solved as in bars 64–68 of the arrangement. What justifies replacing g–d^1 with a^1-e^2?

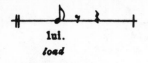

A mar - ché, a beau-coup mar - ché,
March-ing home, march-ing on his way.

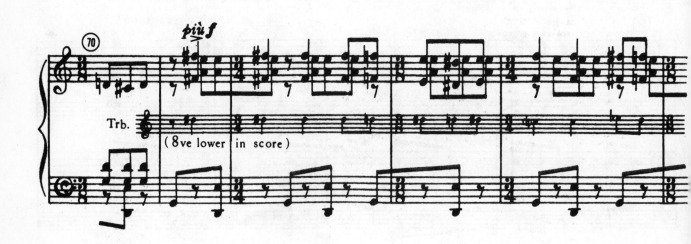

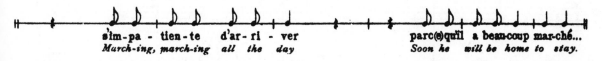

s'im-pa - tien-te d'ar-ri - ver   parc(e)qu'il a beau-coup mar-ché...
March-ing, march-ing all the day   *Soon he will be home to stay.*

Theme With Variations
Second Movement of *Sonata for Two Pianos*
(1943–1944)

Igor Stravinsky
(1882–1971)

In studying this movement, consider what technical and stylistic elements recall the music of earlier periods, and what others announce at once that this is a twentieth-century work.[10] But concentrate particularly on the question, "What is being varied?" Exactly how does the variation technique employed here differ from that of Mozart in the example on page 202?

Stravinsky: *Sonata for Two Pianos.* Copyright 1945 by Associated Music Publishers, Inc., New York. Copyright renewed 1972 by Associated Music Publishers, Inc., New York. Used by permission.

[10]Donald C. Johns discusses this movement in an article in *The Music Review*, (November, 1962), p. 305. See also my article in the same periodical (August, 1968), p. 161.

VARIATION 1

VARIATION 2

VARIATION 3

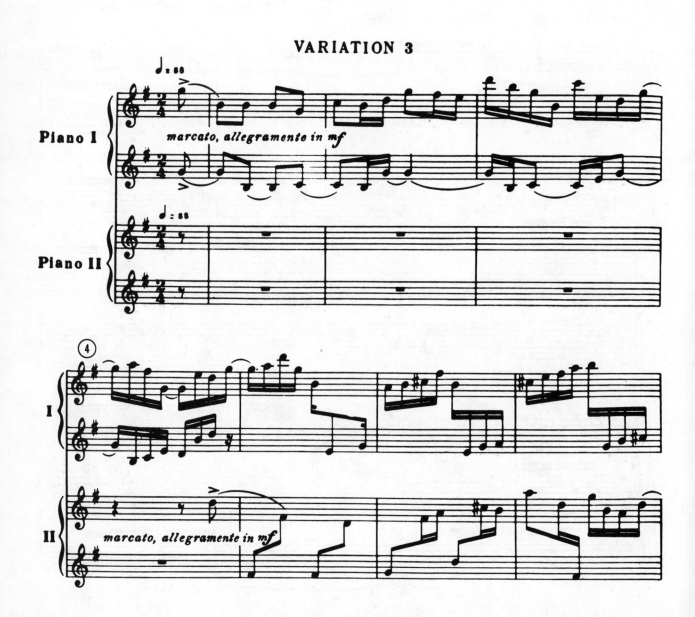

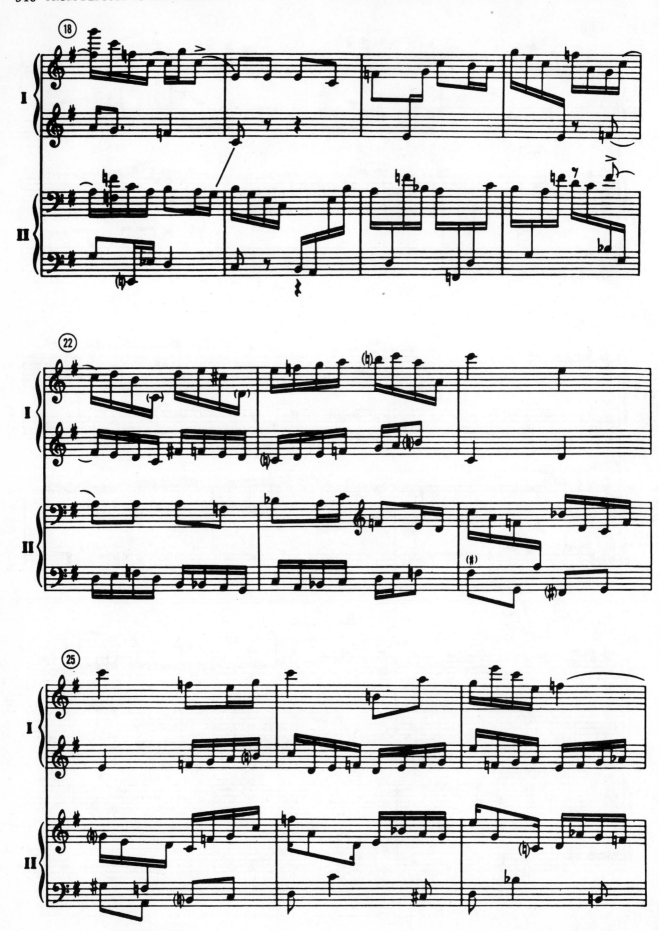

VARIATION 4
conclusion

Five Movements for String Quartet

Op. 5, fourth movement

(1909)

Anton Webern

(1883–1945)

This movement is unified to a high degree by means of repetitions of particular pitches, intervals, and motives. How do special instrumental timbres also contribute to its coherence?[11] A longer "free" atonal work, Schoenberg's Op. 11, No. 1, is given on page 479.

[11]George Perle analyzes this movement in his *Serial Composition and Atonality* (Berkeley and Los Angeles: University of California Press, 1977), 4th ed., pp. 16–18.

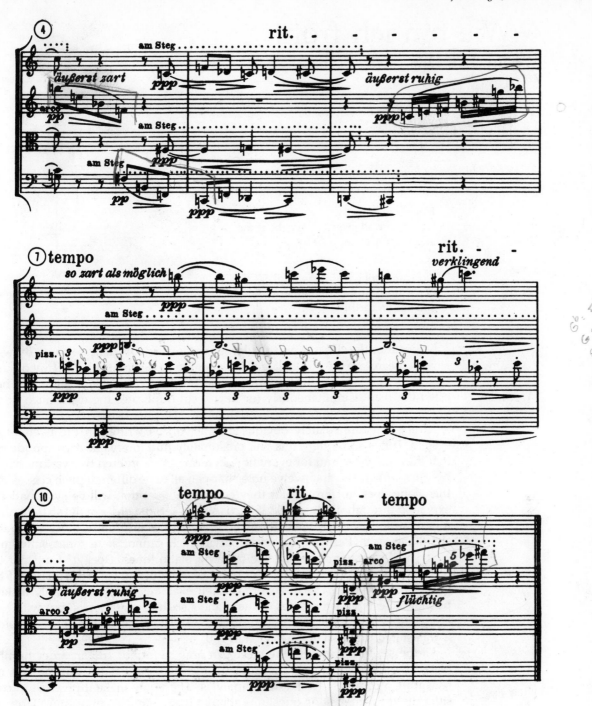

Wie bin ich froh!
No. 1 of *Drei Lieder*, Op. 25
(1935)

Anton Webern
(1883–1945)

Text: Hildegarde Jone

> How joyful I am!
> Once more all grows green about me
> and shimmers so!
>
> Blossoms still cover my world!
> Once more am I at the center of Becoming
> and am on earth.

Notice first the phrases and the larger sections of this delicate song: By what several means are they articulated? Do opening or closing pitches of any phrases or sections reveal audible structural connections? On a smaller level, notice how often the piano simultaneously (or nearly so) duplicates the exact pitch of the voice, producing a quite audible relation between the two.

Rarely is it immediately obvious that a work is written in the twelve-tone system. If it is so written, one will presumably find intervallic correspondences that eventually account for every note in terms of an ordered twelve-tone set. In *Wie bin ich froh!*, the first twelve notes happen all to be different pitch classes, but this alone does not prove that they constitute a set that will be systematically exploited throughout the work. If this is such a set, the order of the sixth to ninth tones cannot be determined from the opening because these tones are stated simultaneously. Perhaps the voice part, which cannot state tones simultaneously, will corroborate the twelve opening piano tones. Does it? Consider the relation of these two sets from the point of view of the basic postulates of the twelve-tone system. The discovery of their exact relation will not only make it possible to establish the order of the piano's sixth to ninth tones, but will leave little doubt that the song is a twelve-tone work. The piano's form of the set, since it was stated first, may be designated P-0.

All the set-forms used in the piece can now be found, and an order-number placed beside every note. (These are always necessary steps, but they do not constitute a complete twelve-tone analysis. They only make it possible to consider the truly interesting questions about a twelve-tone composition.) How are the characteristics of P-0 alone exploited in the composition? How do the various set-forms used in the piece relate to each other? How are these relationships compositionally exploited? How are the above-mentioned simultaneous occurrences of the same pitch in both voice and piano parts accounted for in twelve-tone terms? How is the dispersal of the various set-forms related to the form of the entire song?

These questions, while they, or similar ones, can be asked of many twelve-tone works, of course have been worded here with particular reference to *Wie bin ich froh!* They have very definite answers, which will not only promote understanding of this song, but which, it is hoped, will also demonstrate that an early step in composing a twelve-tone piece is to devise a set whose properties will make possible the kind of piece the composer wants to write.

ca. 1'

Variations for Piano
Op. 27, second movement
(1936)

Anton Webern
(1883–1945)

Examine the sectional form, motives, and dynamics before analyzing the serial pitch-content.

Throughout the piece, the upper staff is to be played exclusively by the right hand, and the lower by the left, notwithstanding changes of clef. What is the relation of each of the hands' parts to the other? Considering this relation, one might imagine that each twelve-tone set-form will be *completely* stated within one hand's part, but this is not the case. To discover the set, write out the pitch classes of the right-hand part until a repetition of a pitch class appears, at which point move to the left-hand part for the remaining notes. Repeat this process inversely, that is, beginning in the left-hand part. In continuing this part of the analysis to the end of the piece, remember that the twelfth note of each set-form also serves as the first note of the next set-form.

Study the progression from each pair of set-forms to the next pair: By what means are the opening two pitch classes, B ♭ and G ♯, arrived at in bars 11 and 22? Consider the way in which all the set-forms used are dispersed over the entire work, as well as the register in which each pitch class of each set-form lies. How much of the work was determined by precompositional decisions? Or, to put it the other way, what elements in the composition are "free?"[12]

[12]Peter Westergaard analyzes this famous movement in his article, "Webern and 'Total Organization,' " in *Perspectives of New Music*, Vol(1963), pp. 107ff. He cites four of the many other writings that deal with it. *See also* Roy Travis, "Directed Motion in Schoenberg and Webern," *ibid.*, Vol. 4, No. 2 (1966), pp. 87–89.

A Swan

from *Six Chansons*

(1939)

Paul Hindemith

(1895–1963)

Text: Rainer Maria Rilke

A foe of atonality and serialism, Hindemith sought to create a musical language that was both contemporary and founded on tonal centers. Wherein does this chanson differ from a work in traditional E minor or E major? By what means is E projected as the tonic? Is the harmony triadic? How is dissonance treated?

A Swan is the second of a set of six chansons for four-part unaccompanied chorus.

> A swan advances on the water,
> Quite surrounded by himself,
> Like a gliding picture.

> Thus, at certain moments,
> A being that one loves
> Is [seen as] a moving space.

> It draws near, doubled,
> Like this swimming swan,
> To our troubled soul,

> Which adds to that being
> The trembling image
> Of happiness and doubt.

A Swan (Un Cygne) from *Six Chansons* by Paul Hindemith. Copyright 1939, 1943 by B. Schotts Söhne, Mainz. Used by permission of European American Music Distributors Corp.

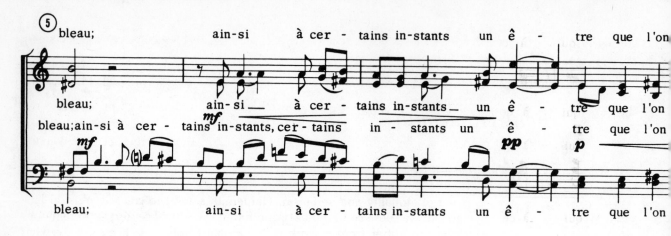

blé-e...qui à cet ê-tre a - jou-te la trem-blan-te i-ma-ge de bon-heur et de dou-te.

blé-e...qui à cet ê-tre a - jou-te la trem-blan-te i-ma-ge de bon-heur et de dou-te.

blé-e...qui à cet ê-tre a - jou-te la trem-blan-te i-ma-ge de bon-heur et de dou-te.

blé-e...qui à cet ê-tre a - jou-te la trem-blan-te i-ma-ge de bon-heur et de dou-te.

Piano Sonata No. 2

First Movement
(1936)

Paul Hindemith
(1895–1963)

What is the tonality of this movement and how is it achieved? Does the dominant-tonic relationship play any part in the projection of the tonality? Is a tonic evident at all times? Is there modulation? A key plan? What relation has the form of this movement to traditional sonata form?[13]

[13]Felix Salzer analyzes this movement in his *Structural Hearing*, Vol. II, Graph 505.

The Banshee

(1925)

Henry Cowell

(1897–1965)

One of the most active avant garde composers of his day, the American Henry Cowell pioneered in the development of new musical resources. In this piece he experimented with novel ways of drawing sound from the piano, and carefully devised a special notation to show the player how to produce the desired effects. (See his "Explanation of Symbols.") He associated these ghostly sounds with a figure from Irish folklore, the banshee, whose eerie shrieks about a house give warning to the family of an approaching death.

One can get no idea of this music from merely looking at the score. It must be played, or heard on the composer's superb recording.[14] The unusual timbres are the most interesting feature, of course, but the pitches have also been carefully worked out. How do the two—timbre and pitch—contribute to the creation of an expressive form?

The score is given on p. 564.

[14]*The Piano Music of Henry Cowell*, Folkways FM 3349.

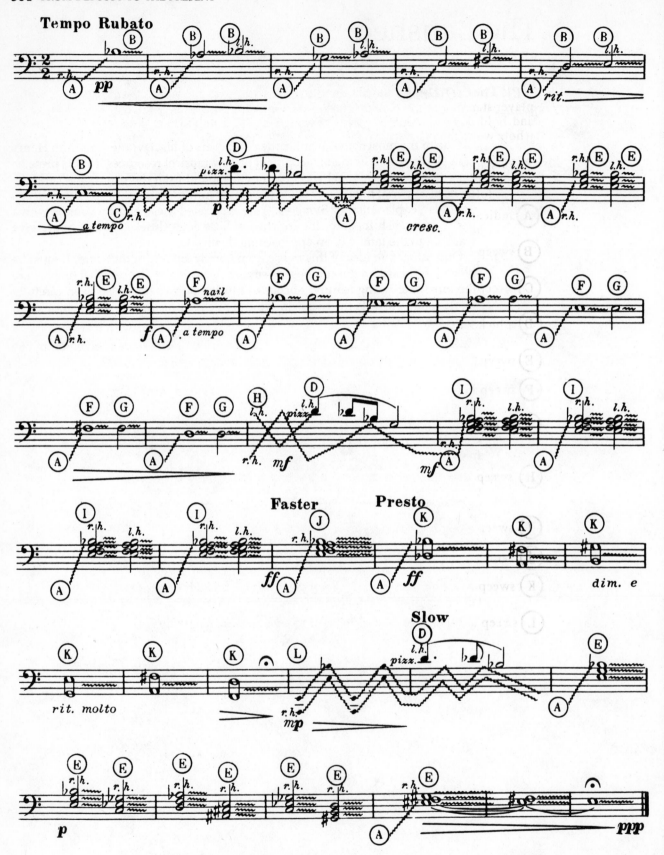

Cowell: *The Banshee* (both pages). Copyright 1930 by W.A. Quincke & Company, Los Angeles, California. Copyright renewed 1958 by Henry Cowell. Copyright assigned 1959 to Associated Music Publishers, Inc., New York. Used by permission.

The Banshee

Explanation of Symbols

"The Banshee" is played on the open strings of the piano, the player standing at the crook. Another person must sit at the keyboard and hold down the damper pedal throughout the composition. The whole work should be played an octave lower than written.

R. H. stands for "right hand." L. H. stands for "left hand." Different ways of playing the strings are indicated by a letter over each tone, as follows:

(A) indicates a sweep with the flesh of the finger from the lowest string up to the note given.

(B) sweep lengthwise along the string of the note given with flesh of finger.

(C) sweep up and back from lowest A to highest B-flat given in this composition.

(D) pluck string with flesh of finger, where written, instead of octave lower.

(E) sweep along three notes together, in the same manner as (B).

(F) sweep in the manner of (B) but with the back of finger-nail instead of flesh.

(G) when the finger is half way along the string in the manner of (F), start a sweep along the same string with the flesh of the other finger, thus partly damping the sound.

(H) sweep back and forth in the manner of (C), but start at the same time from both above and below, crossing the sweep in the middle.

(I) sweep along five notes, in the manner of (B).

(J) same as (I) but with back of finger-nails instead of flesh of finger.

(K) sweep along in manner of (J) with nails of both hands together, taking in all notes between the two outer limits given.

(L) sweep in manner of (C) with flat of hand instead of single finger.

Suite for Violoncello Solo

Op. 84, first movement

(1939)

Ernst Krenek

(1900–   )

Krenek's five-movement suite is based on a single twelve-tone set. In the first movement, the set is used in only one of its 48 possible forms. After placing an order-number beside every note of the piece, consider how the composer has made music of his twelve-tone material. Identify the various melodic ideas, and analyze the form.[15]

Copyright 1942 by G. Schirmer, Inc. Used by permission.

[15]This movement is discussed in Perle, *Serial Composition*, p. 64–67.

Quartina
No. 11 from *Quaderno Musicale di Annalibera*
(1952–1953)

Luigi Dallapiccola
(1904–1975)

This is the final piece of the "musical notebook" that the composer dedicated to his daughter, Annalibera. The eleven pieces, all founded on the same twelve-tone set, are conceived as one large work, and are not to be performed singly.

Quartina, meaning *quatrain*, is an expressive melody with chordal accompaniment. Identify the various set-forms used in the composition. At the first chord of the accompaniment, one cannot immediately tell exactly which set-form is being used, but the subsequent pitches provide the answer. Also, consider possible musical reasons for the choice of the particular set-forms.

Quartina from *Quaderno Musicale di Annalibera* by Luigi Dallapiccola. Copyright 1953 by Edizioni Suvini Zerboni. Used with permission. All rights reserved.

con la massima espressione

(sostenutiss.)

espr.

{m. s.

ppp

ppp

1 min. 20 secondi

Canaries

from *Eight Pieces for Four Timpani (One Player)*
(1950–1966)

Elliott Carter
(1908–   )

This humorous virtuosic take-off on a seventeenth-century French dance is offered here as an analysis problem in rhythm. It abounds in proportional changes of tempo, a device sometimes called "metrical modulation." Merely figuring out the arithmetic is not enough; the study is complete only when the student can give an accurate performance of the rhythm of the piece. Non-timpanists should tap it out on a table top![16]

Canaries is also a study in what can be done with just four pitches. Its over-all form likewise deserves analysis.

[16]Non-timpanists will have enough to do without considering the elaborate performance directions (C, N, R, DS, NS), which refer to ways of striking the drum to produce different timbres. An indispensable part of the composition, these are fully explained in the published set of eight pieces. Pitches notated as an x indicate hand damping.

Etude No. 7

from *Eight Etudes and a Fantasy for Woodwind Quartet*

(1950)

Elliott Carter

(1908–   )

In his *Harmonielehre* (1911) Arnold Schoenberg suggested the term *Klangfarbenmelodie* (tone-color melody) to denote a "melody" produced solely by means of variations in the color, duration, and intensity of a single pitch or chord. The third of his *Five Pieces for Orchestra*, Op. 16, of 1909 had been based in part on this principle (see page 484 of this book); Berg and Webern were among composers to use it later.

Each of Elliott Carter's eight woodwind etudes exploits a particular constructive idea. No. 7 is a study in *Klangfarbenmelodie*. Analyze its form.

Three-Score Set
Second Movement
(1943)

William Schuman
(1910–   )

Polytriads—two (sometimes three) different triads sounding simultaneously—have attracted many composers in this century. In general, are polytriads heard as two separate entities or as a single sonority? What factors affect their color? In this piece, what factors regulate the construction of the polytriads? Does any single tone, triad, or polytriad have priority over the other pitches in the work?

For more complex examples of polytriads, see the excerpts from Stravinsky's *Le Sacre du printemps,* page 523, and *L'Histoire du soldat,* page 532.

No. 1 of Three Compositions for Piano
(1947)

Milton Babbitt
(1916–   )

The earliest twelve-tone theory was criticized because it provided no basis for the control of many of the aspects of composition. For example, it offered nosystematic method for eliminating unwanted pitch-class doublings between simultaneously sounding set-forms. Nor did it provide criteria for selecting the particular set-forms to be used in a given work. Its most signal limitation was that it left unaccounted-for all elements other than pitch. What about rhythm, dynamics, timbre? Because of these inadequacies, attempts were made to develop a twelve-tone theory that, though predicated on the original postulates, would make possible systematic control of all—or, at least, more—of the dimensions of a composition.

One step toward the solution of some of these problems was Schoenberg's discovery that a twelve-tone set could be so constructed that the first six pitch classes (hexachord) of its inversion five semitones higher did not duplicate any of the first six pitch classes of the original set.[17] An example (shown in Figure 1) is the set on which he based his *Klavierstück, Op. 33a.* Inverting this set five semitones higher yields a set the first hexachord of which has a pitch content (though not a pitch *order*) equivalent to the second hexachord of the original (prime) set. The other two hexachords necessarily exhibit the same characteristic. These two set-forms, P-0 and I-5, together with other similarly related pairs, are used throughout the *Klavierstück.*

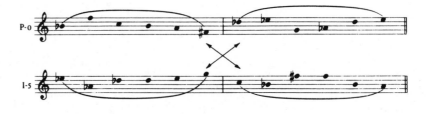

Figure 1

Not all sets operate in the manner described above. The special property of those that do so operate has been termed *combinatoriality* by Milton Babbitt, who has extensively developed the theoretical implications of Schoenberg's discovery. The first of his *Three Compositions for Piano* is based on a twelve-tone set that yields the complex of eight combinatorially related set-forms shown in Figure 2.

Figure 2, with the eight set-forms arranged as four vertical columns of hexachords, shows that any hexachord in the outer columns can be paired with any hexachord in the middle columns without pitch-class duplication. Exactly what is the property of P-0 that produces this result?

[17]See *Arnold Schoenberg, Style and Idea* (New York: Philosophical Library, Inc., 1950), p. 116.

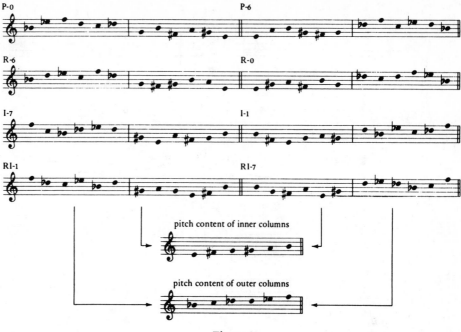

Figure 2

In writing a composition based on the set-complex shown in Figure 2, the choice of which pair of sets to use at a given time need not be haphazard. It is left to the student to discover the pattern of set-forms Babbitt has chosen—a pattern that constitutes one aspect of the over-all form of the composition. No further clue will be given here beyond mention that the movement is in six sections as follows: Section One: bars 1–8; Two: 9–18; Three: 19–28; Four: 29–38; Five: 39–48; and Six: 49–56.

Babbitt has also serialized the rhythm and the dynamics of this composition. Postulating the sixteenth note as the rhythmic unit of reference in his work, he has constructed a rhythmic series the original form of which may be represented by the numbers *5 1 4 2*, or thus:

Establishing the retrograde form of a rhythm is simple enough, but "inverting" a rhythm poses a problem. Babbitt's solution here is to subtract each number of the series from the constant *6*, a process which yields *1 5 2 4* as I and *4 2 5 1* as RI.

By means of brackets we have pointed out in bars 1 and 2 the first expression of the rhythmic series. Here, each subdivision of the series is articulated either by means of holding its last note or by means of rests; these particular holds and rests are variable in length. Other ways of expressing the rhythmic series are used in the subsequent sections of the work. These are left for the student to discover as is also the manner in which dynamics are serially organized.[18]

The *Three Compositions for Piano*, of which only the first is given here, are, according to the composer, intended for performance as a single unit. The following notes to the performer are included in the score: "Accidentals affect only those notes which they immediately precede, except when notes are tied (♯♪‿♪); the following tempi may be substituted for those indicated in the first and third compositions: 96 instead of 108, and 112 instead of 126."

[18]The foregoing is based on an analysis in Perle, *Serial Composition*, pp. 86–87, 99–102, 128–129, 132–134. Fig. 2 is taken directly from Perle.

No piensan en la lluvia, y se han dormido

No. 2 of *Madrigals, Book I*

(1965)

George Crumb

(1929–   )

George Crumb has written four books of madrigals based on fragments from poems of Federico García Lorca. Though each book comprises three madrigals intended to be performed as a group, each madrigal is also a complete composition.

An immediate problem facing the reader of this music is the decipering of its rhythm. Notwithstanding the absence of time signatures and bar lines in much of the piece, the rhythm is quite carefully calculated. The sign ⌐5⌐ means "hold about 5 seconds." At *Molto delicato* and at "Rain-death music II," the pulse is shown by the metronome indication. Is the performer to think (and the listener to hear) the rhythms in these passages in terms of down- and up-beats? That is, do the notes fall into traditional groupings of 2 and 3? The most difficult rhythm problems occur in the two passages that have time signatures: "Rain-death music I" and the overlapping bars of 5 beats each that start at the end of the third system. In both cases the arithmetic is elementary, but performing the rhythms accurately is another matter. How would one conduct these passages? In the first one, how would the vibraphonist get his tempo? Tap out the second passage—the overlapping fives—with two hands on a table top. (See the remarks on Elliott Carter's *Canaries*, page 570.)

Pitch organization in this madrigal also poses analytic problems. As a beginning, notice the four soprano pitches in each of the two *Cristalino* passages, and compare their interval content with that of the bars of overlapping fives. How is the work structured as a whole? Do any single pitches or intervals stand out as focal points of a structural nature? What is the role of timbre in this music?[19]

What does this piece bring that is new? What parts of it are an extension of past practice, different only in degree rather than kind?

[19]The nonverbal vocal sounds in *No piensan en la lluvia* . . . are by the composer and are written in the notation of the International Phonetic System. They are assigned not only to the soprano but to the instrumentalists as well. The vibraphone pitches sound as written. The contrabass pitches, including the harmonics, always sound one octave lower than written; the E string of the contrabass is to be tuned down to E flat.

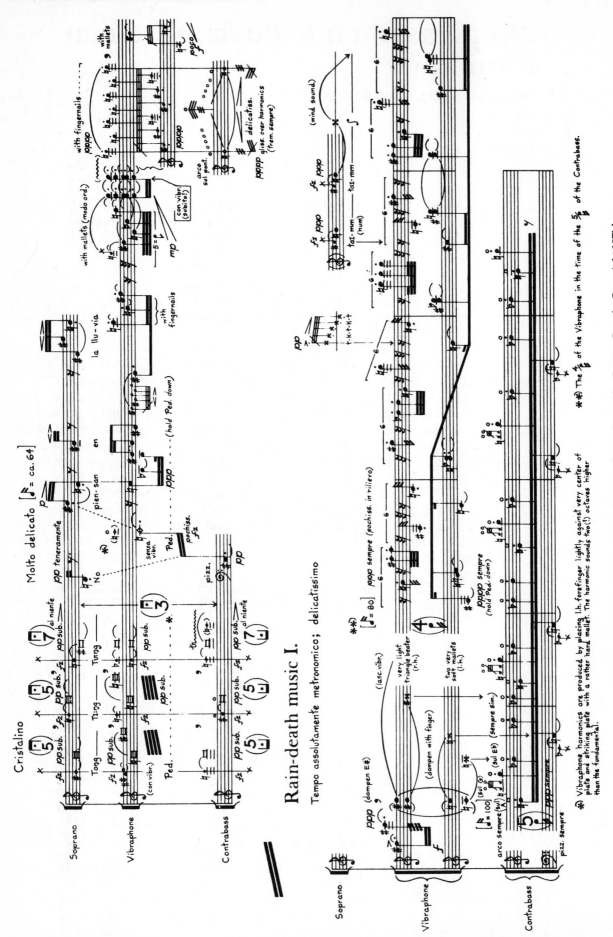

Rain-death music I.

Tempo assolutamente metronomico; delicatissimo

"No piensan en la lluvia, y se han dormido" from *Madrigals, Book I* by George Crumb. Copyright 1971 by C. F. Peters Corporation, 373 Park Avenue South, New York, New York, 10016. Reprint permission granted by the publisher.

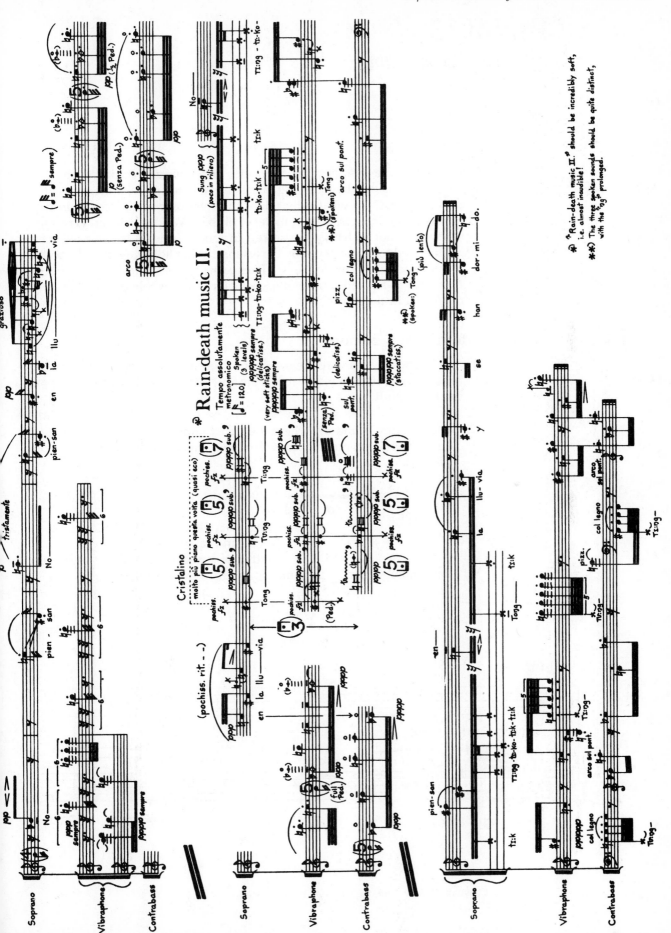

Psalm 13

from *Four Psalm Settings*

(1976–1978)

Bruce Saylor

(1946–   )

After reading the composer's performance directions and getting to know the composition, consider the following questions: Where and how are elements of chance introduced? To what extent does the composer retain control in these places? The flutist must hear the $\frac{4}{8}$ meter of his part. Will the listener? (Try it on a listener who is not watching the score.) In tonal music, is the notated meter always intended to be perceived by the listener? What holds together the pitches of each melodic line? How do the two lines relate to each other? Are any pitches heard as chief in a given phrase or section? Or in the whole piece? How is the text expressed in the music?

Performance Directions

1. The flutist plays in strict time except between bars 37 and 39. The singer, whose part is unmetered, watches the flute part and aligns her part approximately with it.

2. Between bars 37 and 39, where the flutist improvises, the situation is reversed: The flutist now watches the singer's text and interjects the *sf* notes as indicated.

3. Vocal symbols: ●━━━━━ sustained tone;
   ● short tone;
   ◖●◗ reciting tone: Sing the text crisply and rapidly in the rhythm of speech.

4. The symbol + (bar 8, flute) means *slap keys, tonguing sharply*.

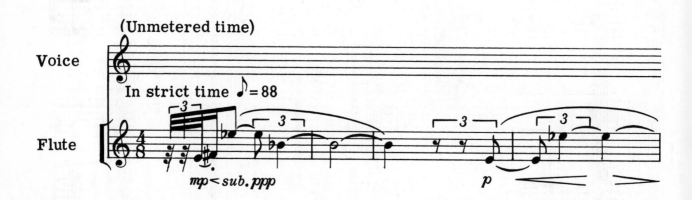

a) Improvise freely and rapidly on these notes, varying the order,
the groupings, and the articulations.

I have trusted in thy steadfast love; ____ my heart shall re - joice ____

in thy sal - va - tion. I will sing unto the Lord because

he has dealt bountifully with me. ____

b) Sing text slowly, choosing
from among these notes.

APPENDIX

Chorale Harmonizations

by Johann Sebastian Bach and several of his predecessors

A chorale is a hymn of the German Protestant church. Starting in the early years of the Reformation, a large body of chorales was gradually developed during the next two centuries. The tunes came from various sources: Some were inherited from Catholic practice, some were contemporary secular tunes for which new, sacred, texts were written, while others were created by Protestant composers. Martin Luther considered them an important aspect of his reformed liturgy, and vigorously promoted their early use. While they were primarily intended for congregations, who sang them in unison, they were soon given elaborate polyphonic settings, and eventually served as the basis of cantatas and organ preludes—a development of great musical importance that extended beyond the period during which the chorales themselves were created and reached its climax in the works of J. S. Bach (1685–1750). (For examples of organ preludes see pages 157–162.)

Chorales are pertinent to the study of harmony and counterpoint not, of course, because of their liturgical origin, or their role in music history, but because their many harmonizations provide a wealth of examples of the basic techniques of four-part writing. The following selection of harmonizations, varying greatly in degree of complexity, is drawn mostly from Bach's cantatas and passions, but also includes several harmonizations and original works by earlier composers. A further aspect of this selection is the inclusion of nine tunes, each of which is given in *two* quite different harmonizations printed one above the other. Both are either by Bach or by Bach and a predecessor. Comparison of such settings can reveal much about unchanging structure on the one hand, and on the other, the techniques of elaboration, with their infinite variety.

In the hymnals of the German church each chorale was usually provided with many stanzas of text. When Bach incorporated a chorale within a cantata or other work, he would select the stanza that best suited his dramatic purpose, then harmonize the tune so as to express the mood of that stanza, frequently even underlining particularly vivid words by some musical device such as an accented dissonance or an unusual chromaticism. For this reason the study of his chorales is not complete without reference to the words. In each of our examples of Bach's harmonizations, we have given the stanza of text he chose in all cases where it is known. Unfortunately, some of his harmonizations have become disassociated from their texts because the large work of which they were a part has been lost. Some of the texts in our selection are given in German, others in English. The latter, always poetic translations of the original stanzas unless otherwise noted, include some that have achieved wide use.

After Bach's death, his son Carl Philipp Emanuel published between 1784 and 1787 a collection of 371 of his father's chorale harmonizations. They were printed without text. To all of them C.P.E. Bach assigned numbers which, though wholly arbitrary, have become traditional. The Bach harmonizations below are identified by their number in the "371." In order to include the pieces by earlier composers, we have arranged all the examples in alphabetical order by title.

Ach Gott und Herr

Melody anonymous, 1625

a) This setting is No. 40 of the "371." Since the work of Bach in which this harmonization occurred is lost, the text he used cannot be known. The first stanza of the hymn is given here. (The original key is C major.)

b) No. 279. This setting is from Cantata 48, *Ich elender Mensch* (1723). Note the text-painting: "Punishment (*Straf*) must follow sins; so let me for them suffer (*büssen*)."

Ach Gott und Herr, wie gross und schwer sind mein be - gang - ne Sün - den! Da

Soll's ja so sein, dass Straf und Pein auf Sün - de fol - gen müs - sen: so

ist nie-mand, der hel - fen kann, in die - ser Welt zu fin - den!

fahr hie fort und scho-ne dort, und lass mich hie wohl bü - ssen!

bü - ssen!

wohl bü - ssen!

Aus tiefer Not schrei ich zu dir

Melody: Martin Luther (?), 1524

a) The text of this chorale, one of the earliest in the repertory, is Martin Luther's poetic paraphrase of Psalm 130. This translation is by Catherine Winkworth (1863). The Phrygian tune, possibly also by Luther, is here given in a 1608 setting by Hans Leo Hassler (1564–1612).

b) No. 10. This setting closes Cantata 38, *Aus tiefer Not* (1724).

Out of the depths I cry to Thee, Lord, hear me, I im - plore_ Thee!
Bend down Thy gra - cious ear to me, My prayer let come be - fore _ Thee!

If Thou re-mem-b'rest each ____ mis-deed, If each should have its right - ful meed,

a)

Who may a - bide _____ Thy pres - - ence?

b)

Christus, der ist mein Leben

Melody: Melchior Vulpius, 1609

No. 6. The text of this harmonization is lost.

Du Friedefürst, Herr Jesu Christ

Melody: Bartholomäus Gesius (?), 1601

No. 42. This setting closes Cantata 67, *Halt in Gedächtniss, Jesum Christ* (1724).

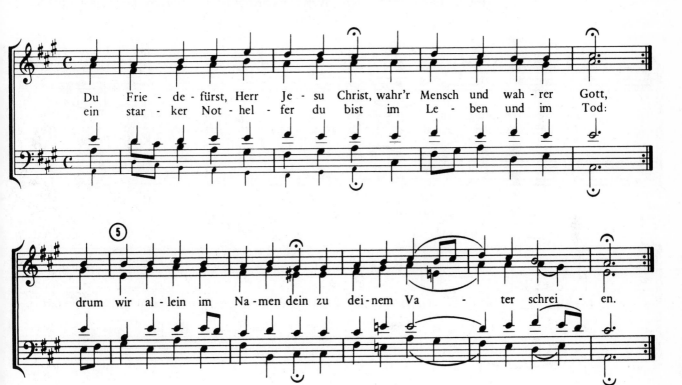

Du Frie - de - fürst, Herr Je - su Christ, wahr'r Mensch und wah - rer Gott,
ein star - ker Not - hel - fer du bist im Le - ben und im Tod:

drum wir al - lein im Na - men dein zu dei - nem Va - ter schrei - en.

Ein feste Burg ist unser Gott

Melody and text: Martin Luther, 1529

Luther's famous Reformation chorale (known in English as "A Mighty Fortress Is Our God") is here given in a harmonization by Hans Leo Hassler (1608).

Ein fe - ste Burg ist un - ser Gott, ein gu - te Wehr und Waf - fen.
Er hilft uns frei aus al - - ler Not, die uns jetzt hat be - trof - fen.

Burg___ ist un -
frei___ aus al -

Der alt___ bö - se Feind, mit Ernst er's jetzt meint; gross Macht und viel List

sein grau - sam Rü - stung ist, auf Erd ist nicht sein's Glei - chen.

Ermuntre dich, mein schwacher Geist

Melody: Johann Schop, 1641

a) No. 102. This setting closes Cantata 43, *Gott fähret auf mit Jauchzen* (1726). This setting is a rhythmic puzzle. It is obvious from the music as well as the text that some first beats of measures do not receive a primary stress. What is the best rhythmic interpretation of this chorale? A performer cannot always be certain how a composer felt a given rhythm, but he must be quite certain how *he* (the performer) feels it. (See also the Hassler composition under *O Haupt voll Blut und Wunden*, page 611', the Dufay *Communio*, p. 18', the last three bars of Bach's *Chaconne*, page 120, and the questions on rhythms in the Bartók pieces on pages 510 and 517.)

b) No. 9. This setting closes Part II of the *Christmas Oratorio* of 1734, where Bach used the ninth stanza of the hymn. This translation is by John Troutbeck (1832–1899).

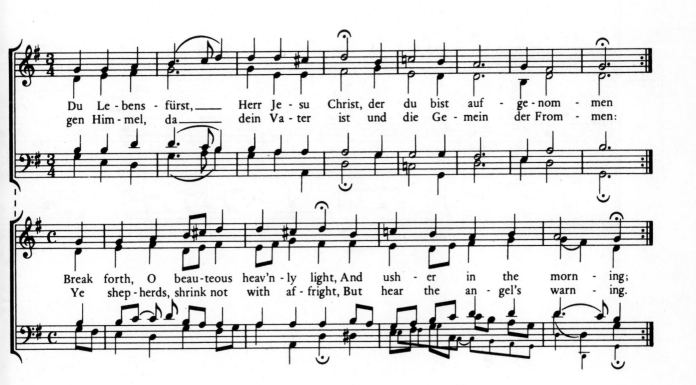

Es ist genug

Melody: Johann Rodolph Ahle, 1662

No. 216. Cantata 60, *O Ewigkeit, du Donnerwort* (1723), concludes with this chorale. Fear of death is finally vanquished by hope in God's salvation. "It is enough: Lord . . . let me rest . . . I journey hence in peace, leave behind my wailing (*Jammer*—see bars 15–16!). It is enough!"

Es ist ge - nug: Herr, wenn es dir ge - fällt, so

span-ne mich doch aus. Mein Je - sus kommt: nun gu - te

Nacht, o Welt! ich fahr in's Him - mels-haus, ich fahr - e

sich - er hin mit Fried - en, mein gross-er Jam-mer bleibt dar-

nie - den. Es ist ge-nug, es ist ge-nug.

Freuet euch, ihr Christen alle

Melody: Andreas Hammerschmidt, 1646

No. 8. Bach closed Cantata 40, *Dazu ist erschienen der Sohn Gottes* (1723) with this setting, which is sung to the fourth stanza of the hymn. The English text given here is a translation by Catherine Winkworth (1863) of the first stanza.

O re - joice, ye Chris - tians, loud - ly, For your joy is now be - gun;

Won - drous things our God hath done. Tell a - broad His good - ness proud - ly,

Who our race hath hon - ored thus That He deigns to dwell with us.

Joy, O joy be - yond all glad - ness! Christ hath done a - way with sad - ness!

Hence, all sor - row and re - pin - ing, For the Sun of grace is shin - ing.

Herr Gott, dich loben alle wir

Melody: Louis Bourgeois, 1551

a) This harmonization by Michael Praetorius (1571-1621) of the tune known as "Old Hundredth" appears in his *Musae Sioniae* of 1609. The original is a whole step higher. In the German church this tune with the text given here was associated with the Feast of the Archangel Michael.

b) No. 164. The work of Bach in which this harmonization occurred is lost. The elaborated bass particularly requires analysis.

für dein Ge - schöpf der En - gel schon,

die um dich schwe - ben in deim Tron.

Herzliebster Jesu

Melody: Johann Crüger, 1640

a) This is a composition of Johann Crüger (1598–1662), a noted writer of German Protestant church music. Many of Crüger's chorales were published simply as melodies with a figured bass. (Figures in parentheses have been added.)

b) No. 59. Bach, who harmonized eleven of Crüger's chorales, made four settings of *Herzliebster Jesu*. This one is from the *St. John Passion* (Part I, No. 7) of 1724. The translation, from the edition of Arthur Mendel, is quite close to the original. Precisely what is the rhythmic difference between Bach's version and Crüger's composition?

was für Mis - se - ta - ten bist du ge - ra - ten?

earth - ly pleas - ures cher - ish, And Thou must per - ish.

Jesu, meine Freude

Melody: Johann Crüger, 1653

No. 263. This was a favorite chorale of Bach, who set it more than once for organ (see page 158), and used it as the basis of his motet of the same name, BWV 227.

Jesu, my joy, my heart's pasture, my jewel,
Ah, how long, how long the heart is anxious and longs for thee!
Lamb of God, my bridegroom, aside from thee
    may nothing on earth be dearer to me.

Je - su, mei - ne Freu - de, mei - nes Her - zens
ach, wie lang', ach lan - ge ist dem Her - zen

Wei - de, Je - su, mei - ne Zier, Got - tes Lamm, mein Bräu - ti-gam,
ban - ge, und ver-langt nach dir!

au-sser dir soll mir auf Er - den nichts sonst Lie-bers wer - den.

O Haupt voll Blut und Wunden

Melody: H. L. Hassler, 1601

a) *Mein Gmüth ist mir verwirret* is a composition of Hans Leo Hassler (1564–1612). A secular song,[1] it was published in Hassler's *Lustgarten neuer teutscher Gesäng* in 1601. Twelve years later sacred words were set to the tune and it entered the chorale repertory. (The original key is D major.)

b) No. 89. This setting is the last of the five appearance of this chorale in the *St. Matthew Passion* of 1729. It occurs immediately after the death of the crucified Christ.[2]

Mein Gmüth ist mir ver - wir - ret, das macht ein Jungk-frau zart, bin
gantz und gar ver - ir - ret, mein Hertz das kränckt sich

Wenn ich ein - mal soll schei - den, so schei - de nicht von mir!
Wenn ich den Tod soll lei - den, so tritt du dann her - für!

[1]"My feelings are all mixed up because of a gentle maid; I've quite lost my way, my heart is sick. I have no peace day and night, I complain constantly, I sigh and weep at all times, I simply despair in my grief."

[2]"When I must depart [this life], then part Thou not from me, [O Christ]! When I must suffer death, then draw Thou near! When deepest sorrows assail my heart, then deliver me from anguish by the strength of Thy anguish and pain!"

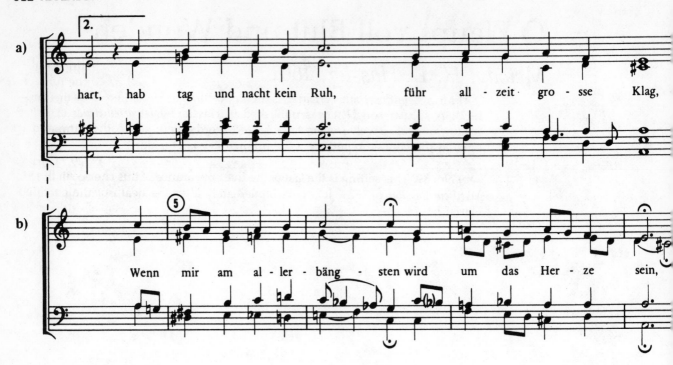

a) hart, hab tag und nacht kein Ruh, führ all-zeit gro-sse Klag,

b) Wenn mir am al-ler-bäng-sten wird um das Her-ze sein,

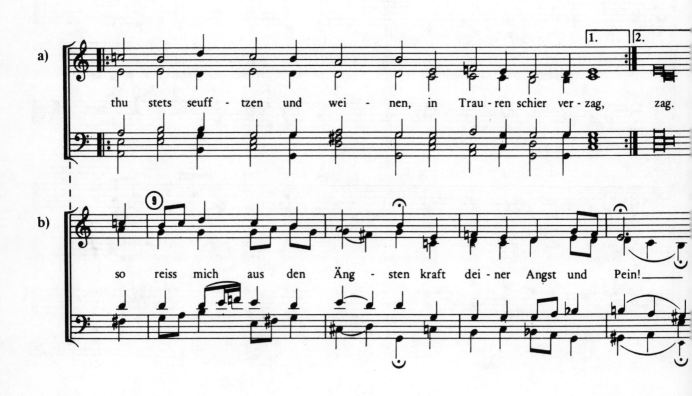

a) thu stets seuff-tzen und wei-nen, in Trau-ren schier ver-zag, zag.

b) so reiss mich aus den Äng-sten kraft dei-ner Angst und Pein!

O Welt, ich muss dich lassen

a) *Isbruck, ich muss dich lassen* (Innsbruck, I must leave thee) by Heinrich Isaac (ca. 1450–1517). It is uncertain whether Isaac composed or borrowed the tune of this secular *lied*. Sacred words (O world, I must leave thee) were set to the tune in 1598. Still another sacred text, *Nun ruhen alle Wälder*, was set to it in 1633. (The original key is F major. We have added the slurs and the tenor's d naturals.)

b) No. 117. This setting is from Part I of the *St. Matthew Passion* of 1729.[3] Christ has just told his disciples that one of them will betray him. They ask: "Is it I?" Then the chorus, symbolizing the contemporary observer responding to the scene, sings this chorale. Bach chose a stanza starting with the words "It is I!"

---

[3]Heinrich Schenker analyzes this setting in his *Fünf Urlinie-Tafeln* (1932), reprinted as *Five Graphic Music Analyses*, New York: Dover Publications, 1969, pp. 32–33.

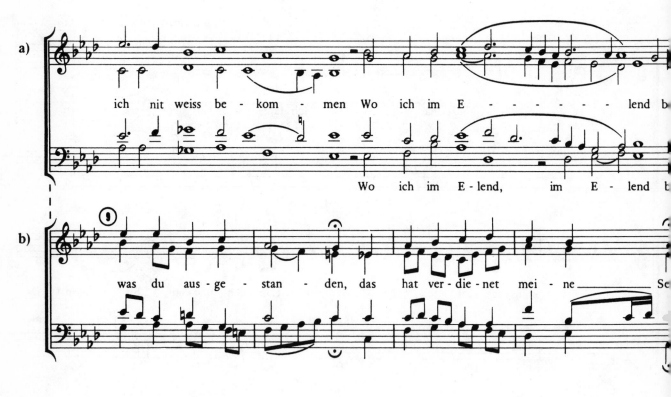

Schaut, ihr Sünder

Melody: M. A. von Löwenstern, 1644

No. 171. The work of Bach in which this harmonization occurred is lost.

Schmücke dich, o liebe Seele

Melody: Johann Crüger, 1649

No. 22.   This setting closes Cantata 180 (1724), which bears the same title as the chorale. Bach uses the ninth stanza of the hymn. The English text given here is a translation by Catherine Winkworth (1863) of the first stanza.

Valet will ich dir geben

Melody: Melchior Teschner, 1613

No. 24. The work of Bach in which this harmonization occurred is lost.

Wer nur den lieben Gott lässt walten

Melody: George Neumark, 1657

a) No. 204. This setting closes Cantata 166, *Wo gehest du bin?* (1724). Bach uses here the first stanza of another chorale, *Wer weiss, wie nahe mir mein Ende.* (The original key is G minor.)

b) No. 339. With this setting Bach closes Cantata 179, *Siehe zu, dass deine Gottesfurcht nicht Heuchelei sei,* of 1723. Again he uses words from another hymn: *Ich armer Mensch.* [4]

[4]"I, poor man, poor sinner, stand here in the sight of God, O'God, deal gently with me, do not take me to task. Have mercy, God of Mercy, upon me."

Wir Christenleut

Melody anonymous, 1589

a)This setting of *Wir Christenleut,* a Christmas chorale, is from the *Cantional* (1627) of Johann Hermann Schein (1586–1630), where it is pitched one half-step higher and bears a signature of one flat. The figured bass is from the original and indicates organ accompaniment. The text is the first stanza.

b) No. 360. This setting is from Part III of the *Christmas Oratorio* of 1734. Bach uses the fourth stanza of the hymn. The translation is by John Troutbeck.

A Note on the Sources

The sources of most of the works of Bach, Beethoven, Brahms, Chopin, Handel, Lassus, Mendelssohn, Schubert, and Schumann are the "critical complete editions" published mostly in the latter nineteenth century by Breitkopf and Härtel of Leipzig. Sources of the remaining works are accounted for either in a permissions notice (on their first page of music) or in the following list.

BACH	*Crucifixus* from *Mass in B minor* (New York: G. Schirmer, Inc., 1899).
BRAHMS	Piano works from *Clavierstücke von Johannes Brahms* (Berlin: N. Simrock, 1879, 1893).
CLEMENTI	*Six Sonatinas* (New York: G. Schirmer, Inc.).
CORELLI	*Les Oeuvres de Arcangelo Corelli*, ed. J. Joachim and F. Chrysander (London: Augener, 1890).
DESPREZ	*Baises moy* edited by Joshua Rifkin from *Canti B numero cinquanta*, published by Ottaviano dei Petrucci, Venice, 1502. The source for the popular melody is Gérold, *Le Manuscrit de Bayeux*, Strasbourg, 1921.
DUFAY	Transcription by Heinrich Besseler in *Die Musikforschung* (Kassel and Basel: Bärenreiter Verlag, 1948), p. 109. Chant source: *Liber Usualis* (Tournai: 1947), p. 1392.
GIBBONS	*Tudor Church Music*, Vol. IV, 1922–1929.
HAYDN	*Piano Sonata* from *Haydns Werke* (Leipzig: Breitkopf und Härtel). *Symphony No. 101* (London: Ernst Eulenburg, n.d.). *String Quartet*, Op. 76, No. 2 (London: Ernst Eulenburg, n.d.).
MONTEVERDI	*Tutte le opere di Claudio Monteverdi*, G. F. Malipiero, ed. (Asolo: 1930), vol. 6.
MOZART	Piano works from the "Urtext" edition published by Breitkopf and Härtel in 1895 with an introduction by Ernst Rudorff. *Piano Concerto*, K. 491 (Leipzig: Ernst Eulenburg, n.d.) *Kyrie* from *Requiem* (New York: G. Schirmer, n.d.).
PALESTRINA	The chant source is an edition of the mass edited by Henry Washington (London: J. and W. Chester, Ltd., 1953). [Compare *Liber Usualis* (1947), p. 235, "On Solemn Feasts."]
SCARLATTI	Ms. 9777, Biblioteca Nazionale Marciana, Venice. A photograph of this Ms. was kindly furnished by Ralph Kirkpatrick. (The notation has been modernized and a few errors corrected.)
SCRIABIN	From an edition by the "Section Musicale des Editions d'etat," Moscow, 1929.
SUSATO	*Musyck boexcken No. 3*, edited by F. J. Giesbert, 1936. (Some erroneous barring has been corrected.)
WAGNER	*Tristan und Isolde*, ed. R. Kleinmichel (Leipzig: Breitkopf und Härtel, n.d.).
WILBYE	The Second Set of Madrigals, ed. G. W. Budd (London: Musical Antiquarian Society, n.d.).
WOLF	All published by Edition Peters, Leipzig, n.d.

INDEXES

The entries in the two indexes that follow refer not to words in the text but to examples of elements in the music. The General Index locates examples of forms, procedures, genres, media, and many devices of both tonal and post-tonal music. The Index of Chords, Sequences, and Modulations is limited almost exclusively to examples from tonal music; it is not alphabetical, but lists the material systematically under "Diatonic" and "Chromatic."

The two indexes are intended as an aid to both teacher and student. For example, a harmony teacher might use the Index of Chords to assign for analysis a passage that contains the particular chord or usage under study. The General Index also isolates a large variety of items suitable for different kinds of presentations and assignments. See, for instance, entries such as "Chromatically descending bass," "Phrase," "Polymeter," "Syncopation," and "Twelve-tone set." Each of these entries—like most of the entries in the Index of Chords—is illustrated not by just one example but by a *group* of examples. One might assign students to look up some or all the examples in such a group, compare them, and select one for performance and discussion at the next class. Study of a group of examples cannot only deepen one's understanding of detail, but also promote a more comprehensive view of a subject by enabling one to see it worked out in a variety of styles from different periods.

When making a selection from two or more examples of a particular entry, it is well to remember that, since such examples are always listed in *page* order, the first one will not necessarily be the simplest or the most suitable for one's purpose. It is advisable to examine the entire group before deciding on the ones to be used.

In the case of forms, genres, and other subjects of large scope, the lists of examples are intended to be complete, but smaller subjects (such as individual chords) are frequently illustrated by only a partial list of the many examples in the book. These have been chosen both for their vividness and to show the most important aspects of a subject. Teachers and students using this book will surely discover many more.

How to Locate the Examples

Numbers in **bold type** refer to pages; numbers in parentheses (   ) refer to measures.

A page number standing alone refers to a complete work and is the page on which measure 1 of that work occurs. For example:

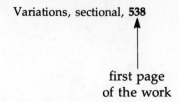

Variations, sectional, **538**

first page
of the work

A page number followed immediately by a measure number (or by measure numbers) indicates the page and the measure(s) where the example will be found, thus:

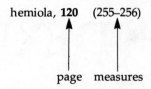

hemiola, **120**   (255–256)

page   measures

In cases where several examples of a particular item are to be found within a single work, all the measure locations are given together within a single parenthesis. In such cases the page number is that of the *first* of the several examples, the rest of which can be readily found by means of their measure numbers only. For example:

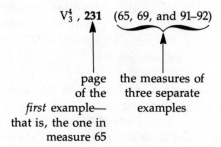

V_3^4 , **231**   (65, 69, and 91–92)

page   the measures of
of the   three separate
first example—   examples
that is, the one in
measure 65

Additional information useful for finding an example is given occasionally in brackets [   ].

General Index

INDEX OF CHORDS, SEQUENCES, AND MODULATIONS

DIATONIC

Chords

The order of the following headings is designed to proceed from simple to complex. The examples grouped under a particular heading will contain not only the chord in question but will often show it in a context consisting of *other* chords. For the most part, such contextual chords are limited to those listed under *earlier* headings.

I, V, and V^7 in root position, **176** (112, 3rd beat–116), **179** (78–80), **236** (173), **239** (44–51), **303** (215–228), **305** (29–34 and 142–156), **377** (1–14), **382** (25–32), **384** (33–40), **418** (1–10)
see also ''Pedal point'' in the General Index.

IV in root position
with I and/or V^7 only, **29** (9–10), **362** (23–26), **380,** (1–4), **383** (6–8),
followed by the cadential $\frac{6}{4}$, **167** (77), **208** [Var. VIII] (3)
pieces using only I, V, and IV, **418, 497** [the hymn]

II, III, VI, and VII in root position (All examples are passages or pieces consisting wholly or largely of triads in root position. Some include V^7.), **27, 28, 180** (123–127), **356** [No. 6] (1–4), **378** (33–40), **441** (41–44), **601** [Version a] (5–8), **606** [Version a], **620** [Version a]
see also ''Cadences, deceptive'' in the General Index for additional examples of VI

Sixth chords
I^6 and II^6 only, **28** (7 and 11), **88** (7 and 10–11), **205** [Var. IV] (15–16), **295** (6, 13–14)
VII^6–I, **34** (9–10), **59** (22), **107** (64), **589** [Version a] (2 and 5), **599** (1), **608** [Version b] (2), **613** [Version a] (1st phrase), **620** [Version b] (3)
6–6–6 (consecutive sixth chords), **18** (5ff.), **170** (22–23 and 107), **275** (59–64), **297** (25–37)

passages or pieces consisting wholly or largely of various $\frac{6}{3}$ and $\frac{5}{3}$ chords, **213** (1–10), **599, 615** (1–3), **616** (1–5), **618** [Version a] (1–2)
see also Sequences (below) involving $\frac{6}{3}$ chords

VII$\frac{5}{3}$ in the major mode, **600** (end of penultimate phrase), **602** [Version b] (9 and 11), **616** (11)

Cadential $\frac{6}{4}$, **58** (16), **144** (8), **167** (77), **176** (111–112), **182** (4), **201** (68), **202** [Theme] (4), **219** (159), **225** (158–162), **283** (15), **385** (29–30 and 46), **442** (62–63)

Other usages
$\frac{6}{4}$ caused by arpeggiation in the bass voice, **263** (521–522), **338** (1), **358** [No. 8] (9, 10, and 11), **395** (76), **431** (7 and 83–84)
$\frac{6}{4}$ caused by neighbor tones, passing tones, or suspensions in upper voices over a stationary bass, **38** (46), **183** (57 and 149), **198** (5), **223** (66–67), **357** [No. 8] (2 and 3), **358** [No. 14] (2), **363** (50), **364** (1), **497** [the hymn] (1)
$\frac{6}{4}$ occurring over a passing tone in the bass voice, **92** (40), **96** (93–94 and 118), **162** (31), **238** (29), **260** (482–485), **277** (66), **599** (8)

Inversions of V^7
V $\frac{6}{5}$, **230** (30), **270** (3–4), **283** (1, 3, 7, 17, 19, 103 and 105), **599** (2), **610** (7),
V $\frac{4}{3}$, **177** (1 and 4), **231** (65, 69, and 91–92), **279** (5, 9, and 42), **286** (78, 95, 98, and 99), **329** (3)
V $\frac{4}{2}$, **85** (1), **110** (14), **217** (111), **221** (72), **236** (176), **286** (71), **375** (17 and 21), **602** [Version b] (8), **605** (11), **606** [Version b] (3 and 14), **613** [Version b] (4)

II^7 and inversions
II^7, **96** (95), **110** (15), **376** (32), **382** (13), **388** (8)
II $\frac{6}{5}$, **35** (35), **38** (44), **71** (2, 4, 16, and 18), **103** (1, 2, and 39), **114** (8), **206** [Var. VI] (3–4), **386** (45), **445** (48), **598** (7), **599** (3 and 8), **605** (2, 4, 6, 10, and 12), **611** [Version b] (3)
II $\frac{4}{3}$, **138** (10)
II $\frac{4}{2}$, **114** (2), **124** (2), **192** (2), **443** (2)

(32), **358** [No. 14] (6 and 16), **420** (11), **444** (22–26 and 30–34)

augmented $\frac{6}{3}$ ("Italian sixth"), **136** (27), **172** (44), **192** (4, 71, 81, and 142 [see also 86]), **207** [Var. VII] (3 and 16), **228** (2), **301** (119–120), **329** (18), **427** (44)

augmented $\frac{6}{5}$ ("German sixth"), **207** [Var. VII] (6), **238** (27), **274** (140), **284** (39 and 86), **294** (185), **342** (41 and 51), **381** (45–51), **411** (10), **452** (10)

augmented $\frac{6}{4}$ ("French sixth"), **282** (73 and 77), **289** (46), **342** (32), **353** (8), **375** [No. 20] (6), **397** (2, 6th beat), **443** (11)

diminished-third chord (e.g., F♯–A♭–C–E♭ [or D] in key of C), **156** (51), **157** (11), **375** [No. 22] (5, 6, and 39)

other chords containing an augmented sixth or a diminished third, **385** (4), **415** (71, 73, 110, and 114), **426** (13 and 45), **451** (1, 6, and 9)

works containing more than one type of augmented chord, **192, 207** [Var. VII], **341**

Sequences

Roots descending in fifths

$\frac{5}{3}$ alternating with $\overset{7}{\underset{5}{3}}$, **138** (13–15), **202** (9), **231** (75–88), **233** (130–136), **272** (68–73)

$\overset{7}{\underset{3}{5}}$ only (successive dominant sevenths), **96** (132–134), **239** (52–55), **309** (112–123), **383** (21–24), **387** (32–37)

$\frac{6}{3}$ alternating with $\frac{5}{3}$, **276** (21–26)

Ascending scale degrees, each preceded by its V in root position, **187** (172–180) [compare **146** (50–56)], **194** (65–67)

6–5 6–5 ascending

each 6–5 a diatonic degree apart, **128** (17–19), **240** (76–81),

295 (33–44), **300** (107–118), **353** (11–15), **621** [Version b] (8–10)

each 6–5 a half step apart, **301** (153–165), **310** (126–133), **389** (25–29)

5–6 5–6 descending, **304** (1–8), **414** (51–57)

7–6 7–6 descending, **96** (129–131), **151** (1–3), **169** (11–13 and 88–90), **186** (146–148), **228** (12–15), **372** (2–4), **426** (28–30)

Sequences a third apart

tonal, **234** (136–139), **293** (158–163), **397** (1–11)

real, **402** (1–5), **412** (31–35), **452** (11–19, piano part), **461** (31–36), **475** (1–3), **515** (40–41), **559** (49–52)

Modulations

Between diatonically related keys, but with salient chromatic voice leading

to the dominant, **179** (81–96), **183** (40–65), **207** (5–8), **423** (1–9)

to the relative major, **156** (49–53), **288** (16–25), **344** (32–58), **608** [Version b] (4–6)

from the relative major back to the original minor, **296** (87–94), **609** [Version b] (9–11)

Between chromatically related keys

tonic triads lying a third apart that share a chromatic half step (e.g., the F♮–F♯ between F–A–C and D–F♯–A), **101** (5–7), **187** (172–189), **304** (14–35), **327** (189–192), **331** (33–45), **332** (80–83, 1st ending), **362** (6–8), **382** (16–20)

tonic triads a second part, **142** (entire), **172** (43–46), **266** (19–20), **346** (72–87)

recitative featuring chromatic modulation throughout, **101**